ECOTOURISM

A Guide for Planners and Managers

Edited by

Kreg Lindberg
Research Associate, The Ecotourism Society

and

Donald E. Hawkins
Director, International Institute of Tourism Studies
The George Washington University

THE ECOTOURISM SOCIETY
NORTH BENNINGTON, VERMONT

Library of Congress Catalog Card Number 93-70175
ISBN: 0-9636331-0-4

Production Director: Megan Epler Wood
Designer: Leslie Morris Noyes, LMN & Co.
Cover Design: Lori J. Johnson, Studio 1-A
Copy Editors: Sarah May Clarkston, Kathleen Lynch
Associate Production Designer: Wendy Guerra

This book was made possible by a grant from the Liz Claiborne, Art Ortenberg Foundation.

Special thanks to International Expeditions for their assistance with the final production of the book.

TABLE OF CONTENTS

Preface

The number of tourists visiting natural areas has increased dramatically in the past several years. Unfortunately, this trend has overwhelmed the ability of many destinations to adequately plan and manage for visitation in what are often ecologically and culturally fragile areas. There have been conferences and several publications concerning ecotourism, but relatively few have focused on the "how to" aspects of planning and management.

The Ecotourism Society is publishing *Ecotourism: A Guide For Planners and Managers* to help fill this void. This publication presents a selection of state-of-the-art planning and management approaches for getting the most out of ecotourism. It is not meant to be the final, comprehensive guide to ecotourism development. Indeed, we hope that it is simply the first in a series of such publications on the subject. We recognize that ecotourism is a broad, interdisciplinary field which involves far more than the topics covered here. In addition, the field is still developing, and we expect continued refinement in methodologies.

We have selected a group of authors who are experts in the ecotourism field. However, the views and opinions expressed by these authors are not necessarily those of The Ecotourism Society. Moreover, the case studies are not presented as an endorsement of what is or is not ecotourism. Rather, they are selected to illustrate specific aspects of ecotourism management.

We would like to thank those who have made this publication possible. The Liz Claiborne, Art Ortenberg Foundation generously provided core funding for the project. And we owe a special debt of appreciation to the authors and reviewers. The reviewers include:

Ray Ashton
Water and Air Research, Inc.

Robert Aukerman
Colorado State University

Miguel Cifuentes
World Wildlife Fund

Thomas Cobb
New York State Department of Recreation and Historic Preservation

John Dixon
The World Bank

Marco Vinicio Garcia

Robert Healy
Duke University

Len Ishmael
Development Planning Services

Rebecca Johnson
Oregon State University

Kurt Kutay
Wildland Adventures

Jan Laarman
North Carolina State University

Boris Gomez Luna
Manu Nature Tours

Craig MacFarland
*Charles Darwin Foundation
for the Galápagos Isles*

Alan Moore
University of Tennessee

Paula Palmer

Art Pedersen

David Richards

Jorge Roldán
*Inter-American Investment
Corporation*

George Stankey
Oregon State University

Geoffrey Wall
University of Waterloo

George Wallace
Colorado State University

Michael Wells

Defining Ecotourism

David Western

Ecotourism has surged through the travel and conservation world like a tsunami, yet its origins are decidedly more evolutionary than revolutionary. Ecotourism's roots lie in nature and outdoor tourism. The scores of visitors who flocked to Yellowstone and Yosemite a century ago were early ecotourists. The first travelers who trickled into Serengeti half a century ago, and the more adventurous Himalayan hikers who camped out on the Annapurna twenty-five years later, were as much ecotourists as the thousands who photograph Antarctic penguins, follow the grouper migration off Belize today, or sleep in Bornean long houses.

The twentieth century has seen a dramatic and continuing change in nature travel. Africa is a good example. Theodore Roosevelt's 1909 hunting safari to bag the biggest heads and horns he could find was a classic of its day. By midcentury photographic safaris were decidedly more popular than hunting trips, though also rooted in the Big Five (large mammals that are popular with game viewers). By the 1970s mass tourism and discriminating tourists, still preoccupied with the big mammals, were ruining habitat, harrying animals, and spoiling the wilderness. Today, such behavior is changing. More visitors are attuned to the harm they can do ecologically, to the value of wilderness, and to the concerns of local people. Specialist tours—birding safaris, camel treks, guided nature walks and so on—are on the rise. This small but growing band is what ecotourism is all about. And, to a surprising degree, ecotourism is making the entire travel industry more sensitive to the environment.

But there is more to ecotourism than a small elite band of dedicated nature lovers. Ecotourism is really an amalgam of interests arising out of environmental, economic, and social concerns. Take conservation, for example. The heady days when the superintendent of Yosemite gloated over the annual visitor entries are gone. In recent years the dangers to natural areas of too many visitors have been a great concern. Conservationists are devoting a good deal of thought to making tourism work for nature preservation.

Tourism has become one of the largest global economic activities—a way of paying for nature conservation and increasing the value of land left natural. How tourist dollars can flow back into conservation and make it pay for itself, or how the nonmonetary value people place on wildlands can be quantified, is a matter at the heart of a new branch of green economics: sustainable development.

And finally, social responsibility. Conservationists, economists, and tourists alike have awakened to the realization that you can't save nature at the expense of local people. As custodians of the land, and those most likely to lose from conservation, locals should be given a fair share. Sound politics and fair economics argue for making local people partners and beneficiaries in conservation, as opposed to implacable enemies of it.

Ecotourism, in other words, incorporates both a strong commitment to nature and a sense of social responsibility. That responsibility extends to the sensitivity of the travelers. The term "responsible travel," another aphorism for ecotourism, encapsulates its aims. The Ecotourism Society gives a slightly fuller definition: "Ecotourism is responsible travel to natural areas which conserves the environment and improves the welfare of local people."

The growing interest in ecotourism among the governments of developing countries, commercial operators, aid organizations, and conservationists speaks to its enormous economic and conservation potential. Ecotourists spend billions of dollars each year. But the importance of ecotourism lies beyond these figures. Ecotourists like to use local resources and local expertise. That translates into import savings, environmentally sensitive designs, and local participation in the travel industry.

Ecotourism's emphasis on local resources and employment makes it attractive to developing countries. Countries rich in wildlands yet disadvantaged by rural poverty and a lack of export earnings are good examples. Kenya earns some $500 million a year in tourism revenues.* The direct and invisible earnings account for some 10 percent of Kenya's gross national product. Tourism income in East Africa as a whole has been the single biggest influence behind its extensive network of protected areas. Costa Rica generated $336 million in tourist revenues in 1991 and registered 25 percent growth in income over the previous three years. Nature-based tourism is the engine of many tropical island economies in the Caribbean, Pacific, and Indian oceans. Ecotourism has put Rwanda and Belize on the map.

Ecotourism is about creating and satisfying a hunger for nature, about exploiting tourism's potential for conservation and development, and about averting its negative impact on ecology, culture, and aesthetics.

Saving nature by selling it is hardly new, but neither are the risks involved in such an enterprise. Yellowstone was sold and saved by constructing a railhead and hotels and advertising the park to a citified nation hungry for the lost frontier. But it wasn't long before the flocks of visitors threatened to love Yellowstone to death. The grizzly—fed, tamed, and turned dangerous on tourist handouts—was one of the

*Unless otherwise indicated, all monetary references in this book are to U.S. dollars.

many victims. Finding the right balance between conservation and tourism has taxed U.S. park planners since the 1940s.

If tourism's good and bad sides are not surprising, the figures associated with tourism certainly are. Four hundred million tourists a year on the move create a welter of problems and challenges unthinkable fifty years ago, as a few examples illustrate.

Ecology. How many visitors can an area absorb? The vulnerability of species and habitats, problems of pollution, waste disposal, and the disruption of critical ecological processes by tourism are barely understood. What is the number of visitors a cheetah can tolerate? What are the limits of acceptable habitat change caused by climbers hacking down the Himalayan scrub for fuelwood? The impact of a burgeoning tourist industry is running far ahead of our ability to measure the damage.

Aesthetics. Impact is measured as much by what visitors will tolerate as by ecological damage. The tourist happy to pay a few dollars to watch a moose in Yellowstone ringed by curious onlookers balks at spending $3,000 to do battle with twenty minibuses around a lion in Serengeti. Values and perceptions complicate the picture. The acceptable levels of use are far lower in Serengeti than Yellowstone because the visitor is paying top dollar for the "feel of the wild."

Crowding ruins the esthetic appeal and lowers the visitor's willingness to pay. Ecotourism reflects a rising set of expectations. If Costa Rica can't offer the feel of the wild, interest will switch to Belize, Guyana, or some yet undiscovered spot. Ecotourism by its very nature builds up expectations and raises the risk of hit-and-run tourism: an influx of nature lovers drawn to the latest wild spot, followed by its abandonment once discovered and degraded.

Economics. It is no longer enough to measure the benefits of tourism in terms of gross or net income. Treating a park as an economic island is unacceptable in poor countries. What about the foreign exchange component or servicing ratio? Is the cost worth the drain on the economy? What about the externalities and opportunity costs of the tourist attracted? And what about the economic dependency and vulnerability tourism brings? Few countries are willing to risk undue dependence on an industry vulnerable to a Gulf War or spate of hijackings. The economics of nature-based tourism is no longer a single column balance sheet.

Social. Culture was the forgotten element in conservation. No longer. Grabbing land for parks is fraught with risks and injustices in a world more conscious of rights and responsibilities. The alienation of local people has become a leading issue in conservation. Conservation and tourism that denies the rights and concerns of local communities is self-defeating, if not illegal. The issues are complex and run deep. Tourism can destroy ancient cultures and ruin indigenous economies. And it takes only a few disgruntled people to disrupt tourism.

The enormous opportunities and awesome risks of nature tourism lie at the heart of the ecotourism mission. Can ecotourism really make any difference to conservation and development on a global scale? Can tourism bring genuine benefits to local communities, draw on local labor and expertise, build locally sustainable markets and bring improvements in health care and education? The answers lie in how we define the mission of ecotourism and the scale at which we tackle the endeavor. Herein lies the dilemma. Only environmentally conscious tourism at low volume is kosher ecotourism, according to many purists.

There is some sense in a restrictive definition. The term ecotourism was, after all, coined for exactly this sort of exclusive nature tourism. But how meaningful would ecotourism be if we stick to a narrow and rigid definition? How much forest can a few well-meaning birders save from ranchers, loggers, and settlers? How many coral reefs can a handful of fee-paying scuba divers rescue from overfishing?

We have to weigh the answer against greater potential inherent in conventional nature-related tourism. Take as an example Amboseli National Park in southern Kenya. Here, over a quarter of a million visitors generate ten times the income produced by Masai from their livestock herds. Tourist income, provided it improves the lives of the Masai and Kenyans at large, is a good reason to conserve wildlife in the entire ecosystem.

Where do we draw the line between low and high volume tourism and between low and high impact tourism? To some extent the co-option of the ecotourist label by virtually any group remotely connected with the nature or culture travel is dictating the answer. Much as we may want to define ecotourism narrowly, in reality the principles applied to the mass market can do more good for conservation—and alleviate more harm—than a small elitist market.

Ecotourism, accepted in this way, is shifting from a *definition* of small-scale nature tourism to a set of *principles* applicable to any nature-related tourism. This is an evolution I think will help conservation. Surely what matters is not scale or motive, but impact. An accidental virus transmitted by a solitary well-intentioned nature lover could threaten the mountain gorilla. A few seeds carried by the mud on a hiker's boot could introduce an invasive weed into a fragile montane ecosystem. By contrast, tens of thousands of environmentally indifferent visitors packing into the aqua dome at Tsavo's Mzima Springs have done little discernible damage and a great deal to save it.

If we accept that ecotourism is about principles of balancing tourism, conservation, and culture, its role is limitless. Yet ecotourism risks floundering in the face of the impossible if we broaden its scope to all nature-related tourism. One way around the dilemma is to start small and aim big—focus on the dedicated nature market and the most pressing issues first. The insights and skills gained can then be scaled up and applied to tourism more generally.

Ecotourism: A Guide for Planners and Managers makes an important start. In it are laid out some of the larger challenges with a series of prescriptions for how to tackle them. These include the tools for looking at demand, use and impact, income distribution, resource inventory, policy formulation, planning, management, training, and local participation.

Ecotourism cannot hope to meet the challenges ahead unless it develops into a professional discipline covering the many interests and skills associated with nature and culture tourism. This is the purpose behind The Ecotourism Society and its latest publication.

Ecotourism As A Worldwide Phenomenon

Héctor Ceballos-Lascuráin

Only a few years ago, the word "ecotourism" didn't exist, let alone the principles it now represents. True, there have been naturalist travelers for a long time, people such as Humboldt, Darwin, Bates, and Wallace. But their experiences were few and far between, so isolated that they did not produce significant socioeconomic benefits to the remote places they visited, nor did their activities seem to be intended as a tool for conserving natural areas, native cultures, or endangered species.

It is only through the advent of jet travel, the enormous popularity of nature and travel documentaries on television, and the rising interest in conservation and environmental matters that ecotourism is truly becoming a phenomenon characteristic of the end of the twentieth century and, hopefully, through the twenty-first.

Tourism in general has already become the most important civil industry in the world. According to the World Travel and Tourism Council (WTTC) tourism is now the world's largest industry, expected in 1993 to generate more than $3.5 trillion of world output, which is 6 percent of the world gross national product. Tourism is a bigger industry than the auto, steel, electronics, or agricultural industries. The travel and tourism industry employs 127 million workers (one in fifteen workers worldwide). Overall, the tourism industry is expected to double by the year 2005 (WTTC, 1992).

Within this perspective, the World Tourism Organization has conducted forecasts of international tourism, which grew by more than 57 percent in the past decade and is expected to grow by 50 percent in this decade. Although the growth rate is slowing, 3.7 percent average annual growth is expected throughout the 1990s, with the 450 million international travelers in 1991 expected to grow to 650 million international tourist arrivals by the year 2000. Nature tourism, in 1989, generated approximately 7 percent of all international travel expenditures, according to World Tourism Organization estimates (WTO, 1992).

Natural areas, and especially legally protected areas, their landscape, wildlife and flora—together with any existing cultural elements—constitute major attractions for the peoples of the countries in which they are found and for tourists around the world. That is why conservation organizations recognize the enormous relevance of tourism and are also aware of the many dangers that badly managed or uncontrolled tourism can cause to the world's natural and cultural heritage.

Ecotourism, as a logical component of sustainable development, requires a multidisciplinary approach, careful planning (both physical and managerial) and strict guidelines and regulations that will guarantee sustainable operation. Only through intersectoral involvement will ecotourism truly achieve its goals. Governments, the private enterprise, local communities, and nongovernmental organizations all have an important role to play. I firmly believe that every country should set up national tourism plans, as part of an integral planning strategy, that include the environmental component and ecotourism guidelines. National ecotourism councils (with representatives from all sectors involved in the ecotourism process) have recently been created in several countries with promising results. Since ours is a constantly shrinking planet (due to modern travel services and facilities, as well as economic and trade agreements), ecotourism strategies can also begin with a regional focus. Different countries could join forces so as to offer attractive integrated packages in the growing world market of ecotourism services.

Chronic problems, such as underbudgeting and understaffing of many protected areas, especially in developing countries, could finally begin to be solved if adequate mechanisms for pumping tourism dollars into national park systems were set in place. Also, the alarming poverty in many rural areas around the world could perhaps be alleviated if the right formulas were reached for involving local communities in the ecotourism process.

An important point to emphasize is that ecotourism should not be restricted to legally protected areas, since too much pressure could eventually be exerted on them. Promoting ecotourism in natural areas that have no official protection may foster effective action from local populations to conserve their surrounding natural areas and resources out of self-interest, and not because of external constraints.

Ecotourism is a complex and multidisciplinary phenomenon. There are many facets that must be addressed if it is to be successful for those involved: consumers, managers, native peoples, and suppliers. Detailed and systematic inventories of the ecotouristic attractions (both natural and cultural) of a country, a region, or a site should be elaborated, bearing in mind that these inventories are different from those of a scientific nature, and that they should reflect the attractiveness of the features listed (and not merely constitute an unemotional and clinical description of their biological or archeological significance).

The training component is vital. Courses and seminars directed to different audiences (tour operators, field guides, hotel owners, park managers, local community groups, government planners) are urgently required. Training programs should be of a practical nature, combining classroom activities with field practice.

Adequate physical facilities in and near natural areas are required for the effective development of ecotourism. Appropriate planning, design, and building criteria must be applied, minimizing impact on the environment, providing for a certain degree of functional self-sufficiency, and adding to the quality of the visitor's experience. Interpretive centers are sadly lacking in most protected areas of developing countries. Special attention should be addressed to providing facilities which are attractive, pedagogically appropriate, and easy to operate and maintain, always in accordance to the social and economic reality of each case. Since many protected areas are located in sites of difficult access, and far from traditional services, it is wise to apply what is loosely termed as "ecotechniques," such as solar energy (for heating water and/or providing electricity), capture and reutilization of rainwater, recycling of garbage, natural cross-ventilation, and the use of native building materials and techniques. Buildings, roads, nature trails, signs, observation towers and blinds should all be carefully designed so as not to abruptly interfere with the environment, as well as serving to enhance the visitor's experience.

Many conferences and symposia have been held on the vast subject of ecotourism since 1990; the interest of government officials is now widespread. In many parts of the world, private investors are also turning their attentions to this phenomenon. The time has come to act on a practical basis, setting up concrete and realistic projects that may demonstrate the potential and true benefits which are so often being proclaimed. This book offers an excellent introduction to a whole new era of ecotourism implementation.

REFERENCES

World Tourism Organization. 1991. *Yearbook of Tourism Statistics*. Madrid, Spain.
World Travel and Tourism Council. 1992. *The WTTC Report: Travel and Tourism in the World Economy*. Brussels, Belgium.

Ecotourism Planning
for Protected Areas

Elizabeth Boo

Ecotourism has dramatically captured the attention of many people. Protected area managers are trying to accommodate increasing numbers of visitors to parks and reserves. Communities near protected areas are experiencing new employment opportunities through tourism. Rural development specialists are investigating ecotourism's economic potential and governments are considering it as a source of foreign exchange. Tourism bureau officials are beginning to create ecotourism policies; private sector funding agencies are evaluating the financial viability of ecotourism investments. The tourism industry is booming with new nature trips, dubbed ecotourism. Travel writers are trying to get the latest word on this innovative concept; ecotourism videos are abounding. And, of course, travelers—the primary drive behind all of this enthusiasm—are becoming more adventurous, more nature-oriented, and more participatory when they travel. Travelers are visiting parks and reserves worldwide like never before and are looking to these experiences as a way to get to know and appreciate the natural environment.

And what are conservationists' interests in this ecotourism boom? Conservationists want to determine if ecotourism is a legitimate tool for preserving biological diversity and promoting sustainable development. This hypothesis needs to be validated or rejected through case studies.

There is a high level of expectation among ecotourism managers about what ecotourism can produce. There is also a great deal of concern about the challenges it creates.

The theoretical impact of ecotourism is well-known. The potential *costs* are environmental degradation, economic inequity and instability, and negative socio-cultural changes. The potential *benefits* are generation of funds for protected areas, creation of jobs for people who live near protected areas, and promotion of environmental education and conservation awareness.

Given these potential costs and benefits, there are mixed feelings about ecotourism. We see both opportunities in ecotourism that may advance our efforts, and problems with ecotourism that may hinder our work. Our job now is to see where ecotourism intersects with conservation and development work, and to identify ways to minimize its costs and maximize its benefits.

There are several areas where ecotourism intersects with conservation efforts. At World Wildlife Fund (WWF), these areas are: protected area management, sustainable development in buffer zone areas, environmental education for consumers, and influencing policy decisions.

One of the most urgent points of intersection is in protected area management. The current situation is troublesome. Protected areas worldwide have seen increased visitation levels. Some of these increases are dramatic—doubling or tripling in a year—and many of these areas are not prepared for tourism. They are staffed by people who are not trained in tourism management.

In addition to facing these new management challenges, these same parks are underfunded, understaffed, and experiencing a multitude of development activities in and around their borders. All of these factors are threatening the conservation of protected areas. Some of these threats could be alleviated if the potential benefits of tourism could be harnessed. Fortunately, the majority of ecotourists are eager to contribute more than is currently being requested to conserving the areas that they visit. People want to play a bigger role in conservation when they travel. However, the opportunities must exist to allow them to contribute. Examples of these opportunities are entrance fees system, locally owned and managed lodges, or native handicrafts cooperatives. In order to provide these opportunities, systems must be in place. And this requires planning.

So, how does a protected area plan for ecotourism? Where are the examples? Where are the models? Where are the guidelines? In recent months WWF has received many requests from protected area managers for assistance in creating ecotourism plans for their areas because there is so little information about where ecotourism works and how to do it. Our response to these requests was to write "Ecotourism Diagnostic and Planning Guidelines" specifically for protected area managers. This document is part of the WWF Wildlands and Human Needs series of technical papers.

"Ecotourism Diagnostic and Planning Guidelines" is an effort to help parks determine their relationship with tourism. It is still undergoing testing and refinement. Our first case study using this diagnostic is in the Blue Mountain/John Crow Mountain Reserve in Jamaica. To date, phase one of the planning process is completed.

The "Ecotourism Diagnostic and Planning Guidelines" can be used as a thought piece to help protected area managers evaluate the issues of ecotourism. Or the diagnostic can be used as a tool for a more formal planning process that would result in an official ecotourism strategy for the area. The scope of the document is limited. First, it assumes a manager for the area, and thus is intended for areas that have protective status. It does not cover "virgin" territories outside protected area systems, though these areas are also experiencing increased tourism. Second, the document provides a framework for a planning process but does not detail how to implement each section. For example, to actually create an ecotourism strategy, planners will need further assistance in the mechanics of developing a business plan. They will also need information regarding construction of environmentally-sound infrastructure and facilities. This diagnostic is meant to be used in conjunction with other resources.

The document will soon be accompanied by a similar one on ecotourism planning for local communities and a third planning document geared toward governments will follow. Together, these three planning tools will hopefully allow regions to coordinate planning efforts for ecotourism.

We do not yet know the conservation and sustainable development value of ecotourism. Nor do we know to what extent its benefits can be maximized and its costs minimized. But, we do know that without planning and management, ecotourism will not succeed. This chapter is a summary of an initial planning process to help parks prepare for tourism.

SUMMARY OF "ECOTOURISM DIAGNOSTIC AND PLANNING GUIDELINES" FOR PROTECTED AREA MANAGERS

Many parks and reserves are facing rapidly growing levels of visitors. The vast majority of protected areas are unprepared for this consumer trend. Many of these areas were not designated or designed as tourism sites and lack adequate funds and staff to meet the needs of increasing numbers of nature travelers. Since most protected area managers have neither prepared nor planned for tourism, they are now facing the urgent challenge of managing tourism growth so that it can benefit both the park and surrounding communities.

In response to rising ecotourism trends, protected area managers need to evaluate what level of tourism is best for each area and then devise a strategy to achieve that level. The strategy will guide the development and management of ecotourism to ensure that the protected area is not overrun and destroyed by tourists, to establish mechanisms to generate employment and revenue for the protected area and surrounding communities, and to create opportunities for environmental education for visitors. An ecotourism development and management strategy will allow protected areas managers to either encourage or discourage ecotourism as appropriate, both in terms of numbers and activities. The following guidelines are designed as a tool to assist park managers in the process of creating this strategy. With a strategy in place, parks and reserves can minimize the costs of ecotourism and maximize its benefits.

The objective of the "Ecotourism Diagnostic and Planning Guidelines" is to create an ecotourism strategy for protected areas that want to better manage tourists. Better management may involve either promoting or limiting tourism in the area.

STRATEGY

This strategy has three phases.

First, to assess the current tourism situation and potential. What is the status of the natural resources? What is the level of tourism demand and development? Who benefits from tourism? What are the costs? What is the potential of tourism development?

Second, to determine a desirable tourism situation and identify steps to reach this situation. Decide what is the best level of tourism for the area. This decision should reflect a balance among the needs of visitors, natural resource, surrounding communities, and host governments. Once a decision is made, determine what needs to be done, what skills are required for each task, who will do what, how long it will take, and how it will be financed. Prioritize these activities.

Third, write an ecotourism strategy document. Document the ecotourism strategy, publish it, and circulate it to potential sources of financial and technical assistance and other interested parties.

These three phases (each of which will be described briefly in the following sections) constitute the process of creating an ecotourism strategy for a protected area. Once the strategy is in place, its activities need to be actualized. This will require a great deal of work in some cases.

PHASE ONE: ASSESS THE CURRENT SITUATION

Ecotourism development and management is a significant natural resource management issue that many protected area managers face. Therefore, phase one of the diagnostic begins by looking within the park itself (for simplicity, the term "park" will be used to refer to any type of protected area—national park, private reserve, biosphere reserve or other). The first section deals with features inside the park boundaries. Issue areas are natural resources, park infrastructure, visitation, and park personnel. Park personnel are generally in charge of overseeing these areas as part of their job responsibilities.

There are other issue areas, not in the park managers' immediate jurisdiction, that also directly or indirectly impact tourism within the park. These issue areas may be local, regional, national, and in some cases, international in scope, and will be covered in the section entitled Bridges Outside the Park Boundaries. That section will examine the interaction with local communities (local); regional infrastructure; other attractions (regional within the country); legal, policy, and budgetary issues (national); and involvement with the private sector (local, regional, national, international).

For example, on a national level, most protected areas belong to a park system and are generally governed by national laws. Individual park managers may feel that national park laws are outside of their jurisdiction, but it is important they know which laws impact tourism within their park and decide if there are any that they can influence to improve the tourism situation within their park. Although changes may only come through a national level legal process, park managers need to understand how the process works, who the decision makers are, and how they can influence the process. This same principle applies to local, regional, and international issues.

Information for phase one of the process can be obtained through original research, interviews, and collection of data from secondary sources. Potential sources of information include park officals and personnel, government officials and records, local communities, private sector and tourism industry representatives, and conservation organizations. Hiring an independent researcher to write a report for this phase may be useful.

The following is a series of questions that will serve as guidelines for assessing the current tourism situation. These questions are intended as a framework to stimulate the thinking process. In many cases, they will need to be modified to fit particular situations within parks. There may also be other questions that are appropriate to add to the list.

In writing a report on phase one of the diagnostic there will be some subjectivity on the part of the researcher, but the goal is to be as objective as possible. Therefore, in answering the questions below, there are several words that will have to be defined by the researcher in the local context. In this way, the participants will use the same definitions and have the same information at the start.

FEATURES INSIDE PARK BOUNDARIES

The following questions have to do with the park's natural resources.

- Why was the park established? There may be various opinions in response to this question. If so, note and reference.

- Give a brief description of the natural resources in the park. Are the resources intact or are they threatened? (Define threats in the local context.) Threats are generally those things that affect a species' ability to reproduce and survive. They may include tourism, logging, mining, slash-and-burn agriculture, poaching, etc. Explain.

- What inventories or studies of the protected area's flora and fauna have been conducted? Inventories may be studies about biogeographic areas or individual species. Topics may include forest types, birds, entomology, mineral resources, and hydrology issues.

- Which of these inventories are relevant for ecotourism planning in the park? Include a brief review of those that are relevant and why they are useful.

- What sites and/or wildlife are the biggest current and potential tourist attractions in the park? Why are they attractions?

- Do any of these sites have fragile (define) natural resources? Is any of this wildlife endangered or threatened? Explain.

- Have any attempts been made to quantify the impact of tourism on these resources? Cite and review these studies. If no formal studies exist, is there any anecdotal information available?

- Are studies available that describe the impact of tourism in other parks, which might be useful to this case?

The following questions have to do with visitation information and levels.

- Is there a system for recording visitor statistics in the park? If so, describe it.

- How many people visit the park each year? (Estimate if no records exist; indicate if figure is estimation.)

- What is the ratio of foreigners to nationals?

- What other demographic information do you have about visitors? (Examples: age, specific country of origin, etc.) If this has not been recorded officially in the park, perhaps lodge owners and tour guides have statistics or anecdotal information that would be useful.

- What are the high/low seasons of visitation? Why?

- What do visitors do in the park? List the activities and indicate the most popular ones.

- What surveys have been conducted regarding visitation in the park? What were the results?

- What is the average amount of money that tourists spend in the park? (Approximate if no official figures exist.) Where do tourists spend their money in the park?

- What kind of promotion or marketing schemes has the park pursued to attract visitors? Collect relevant brochures and marketing pieces and attach to the phase one report.

- What level of visitation can be realistically expected for the future?

- What market does the park serve, actually and potentially (local visitors, mass foreigners, elite foreigners, other)? How does this affect the type of visitor experience and infrastructure that is desired?

The following questions have to do with park infrastructure.

- List all infrastructure in the park. (Examples: visitors center, trails, restrooms, restaurant/snack bar, gift shop, and lodges.)

- Are these facilities used? How frequently? By whom? List separately.

- Describe the facilities. Are they old or new? Are they maintained? Who is responsible for their maintenance?

- Are facilities owned by the park service, private sector, or other? If the private sector is involved, are they local, national, or foreign? Specify each case.

- Which facilities/infrastructure contribute to environmental education for visitors? (Examples: interpretive signs on trails, information brochures in visitors center, videos.)

- What kinds of educational materials are available in the park? Describe them.

- Who prepares and produces these materials? What are the audiences?

- How are the educational materials distributed? Are they useful?

- Which facilities/infrastructure within the park contribute financially to the park? (Examples: gift shops, entrance fee systems, snack bars.) How? Can the financial gains to the park be quantified for each?

- Which facilities/infrastructure within the park contribute financially to surrounding residents? (Examples: gift shops, restaurants, lodges.) How? Can the financial gains to local residents be quantified for each?

The following questions have to do with park personnel.

- How many park personnel are directly involved with tourists? What are their jobs? Are they volunteer or salaried? What is the funding source for salaries?

- What type of training did park personnel receive to work with tourists? Explain.

- Is the number of park personnel adequate for the level of tourism? Can they adequately protect the natural resources of the park? Explain.

BRIDGES OUTSIDE PARK BOUNDARIES

The following questions concentrate on interaction between the park and local communities.

- Identify local individuals, communities, and nongovernmental organizations involved with/affected by tourism to the park. List separately. For those involved with tourism, is it on a full-time or part-time basis?

- What are the costs and benefits of tourism for these people? Specify for each. Costs may be competition for land use, destruction by wildlife, undesireable cultural interaction, and others. Benefits may be financial gain, employment, environmental education, and so on.

- Identify types of tourism businesses or other products and services that involve the local population.

- For products and services sold through independent or informal channels list kinds of products and services sold, method of selling, estimatepercentage of market share these informal vendors have, methods of promotion, and any other relevant information.

- Who owns or has access to the means of production in each of these cases?

- Are there any tourism cooperatives or associations in the area? Who belongs? What do they do? Are they effective?

- For those residents of local communities not involved with tourism in the area or for those only involved part-time, what other kinds of economic activities/employment do they pursue?

The following questions deal with regional (within the country) infrastructure.

- How accessible is the park? Describe its location and the surrounding region.

- How do foreigners normally transport themselves to the park? How do nationals normally get to the park?

- What is the condition of the roads? Are there seasonal difficulties (rainy season, other)? Who is responsible for maintaining the roads?

These three questions inquire about other regional attractions.

- What other tourist attractions exist in the region? (These may be historical, cultural, natural, events, or urban.) List each separately and the number of visitors annually. Which of these are bigger attractions than the park itself?

- Are there any existing "tour packages" that include the park as a part of a larger trip itinerary? Are there any other interactions between the park and the other tourism attractions in the region?

- What are the population centers within 150 kilometers of the park? List city (town), number of residents, and distance from park.

The following questions take a national perspective, such as legal framework, policy considerations, and budgetary issues.

- What are the existing (or proposed) legal documents that regulate tourism activities in the park?

- What specifically are the rules and regulations in these documents for tourism activities? Cite them.

- What are the objectives of tourism to the park?

- Is there a tourism section in the park management plan? If so, is it effective? If not, what are the constraints?

- Does the park have zones for certain activities? Is there a tourism zone?

- Who is responsible for establishing and monitoring tourism policies in the protected area—the park service, tourism officials, others? If more than one group is responsible, do they work independently or jointly? Is this effective? If not, why not?

- Is there a system for collecting entrance fees at the protected area? If so, describe it. If not, why not?

- Does the income from the entrance fee system go into the central government funds or stay in the protected area? Explain the process.

- What is the source of funding for the national park service? (For example, the national treasury, outside donors, trust fund or endowment.)

- Is this funding adequate for the current tourism management activities? Is there funding available for future tourism management activities?

- How is the overall protected area budget divided among individual parks and reserves?

The following questions concern private sector involvement.

- How is the private sector involved with tourism in the park?

- Does the park collaborate with any particular tour operators or companies? Are they foreign or national? Does the park have any exclusive relationships?

- How does the park select the tour operators/companies with whom it will work?

- Has the private sector been involved in any conservation related projects in the park or surrounding area? Describe.

- Does the park/government have any policies or regulations regarding private sector involvement in the park?

PHASE TWO:
DETERMINE DESIRABLE TOURISM LEVEL AND CREATE A PLAN

Phase two is a workshop (or set of workshops) to bring together a diverse group to analyze the current tourism situation in the park, decide how it may be improved, and create a plan for improving it. The tourism situation may be improved by increasing or decreasing the number of tourists, changing when they come and what they do, improving the facilities and services offered, offering further protection to the natural resources, or expanding the beneficiaries of tourism. It is important for participants to be very creative in this process.

In order to decide how to improve the tourism situation in the park, the group must first evaluate the objectives of tourism to the park. Objectives may include offering a new form of protection for the resources, bringing foreign exchange into the country, offering environmental education to national and international visitors, and creating new employment opportunities for surrounding communities.

Based on this discussion, the group will strive to reach a concensus on the desirable number and activities of tourists in the area. This should reflect a balance of many concerns, such as conserving natural resources, promoting sustainable development in local communities, improving the national balance of trade, and enhancing the tourists' experience. Once the group has reached a concensus on the profile of tourism to the park, an ecotourism strategy must be created. This will be an action plan outlining necessary steps to achieve and manage the desirable level of tourism.

The strategy will include a list of activities needed to develop ecotourism in the park. These activities might involve training park guards in tourism management, building a visitors center, hardening sites to reduce damage from visitors, setting up an ecological monitoring system, printing promotional brochures, developing a handicraft cooperative with local communities, lobbying the government to establish an entrance fee system with funds going directly back to the park, and selecting tour operators to bring groups to the park. The strategy should detail activities in priority order and describe the skills needed to do the task, identify who will manage/perform the activity, how long it will take to complete, and how much it will cost. In this way, it will be clear to potential funders how the park wants to see ecotourism develop. In determining priorities, it may be important to consider if there are any areas of the park that are most threatened by tourism which would require urgent attention.

In addition to actually carrying out the strategy, a monitoring system for the strategy must be established. There must be some procedure for soliciting feedback on the strategy, evaluating its impact, and for modifying or adjusting it as necessary. A strategy is a dynamic process.

METHODOLOGY

Since there are many issues involved in determining ideal tourism development for the area, many groups must be represented in the discussion. There should be representatives from the park, the surrounding community, the tourism industry, the ministry of the environment or natural resources, the ministry of tourism, and the conservation community. A facilitator will be useful for these meetings.

There are four objectives for the workshop (or set of workshops).

- The first is to bring representatives from many sectors together to share goals for the development of the ecotourism industry in the park.

- The second is to build a coalition among groups to form an ecotourism committee for the park.

- The third is to identify the preferred ecotourism development scenario for the park.

- The fourth is to determine a strategy for pursuing this scenario.

FEATURES INSIDE PARK BOUNDARIES

One of four desired components of the strategy will consider the park's natural resources.

- Set up mechanisms to monitor the ecological impact of tourism. It may be useful to gather information from other sites about how to do this. List the skills needed for this project, who will do the monitoring, how long it will take to research and set up, and how much it will cost.

- Conduct inventories for wildland sites, ecosystems, or species that have not been adequately studied. This is particularly important for those that are or will become tourism attractions. List the skills needed for this project, who will conduct the inventory, how long it will take to complete inventories, and how much it will cost.

Another desired component of the strategy will consider visitation information and levels.

- Create a system to record visitor statistics. This should include not only numbers, but demographic information. List the skills needed for this project, who will do it, how long it will take to set up a record system, and how much it will cost.

- Plan a series of visitor surveys. Survey questions will fill in the data not included in the visitor record system and give important marketing and management information. This includes questions such as: What do you like and dislike about the park? How did you hear about the park?, etc. List the skills needed for this project, who will be in charge of the surveys, when they will occur, and how much it will cost to conduct surveys and process information.

The third desired component of the strategy will consider park infrastructure.

- Create a master plan of all existing and proposed infrastructure in the park. This will include trails, signs, facilities, and more. Consult with experts to get the latest designs in ecologically sound structures using local materials. List the skills needed for this project, who will be in charge of the master plan, how long it will take to create, and how much it will cost.

- Once the master plan is complete, list the priority activities (either improving existing structures or building new ones), identify appropriate architects and builders, and begin construction. Ensure that local products and services are used to the extent possible. List the skills needed for this project, who will be in charge of coordinating construction, how long each project will take, and how much each one will cost.

The fourth desired component of the strategy will consider human resources available to the park.

- Decide what skills and corresponding park personnel are necessary to manage desirable level of tourists. This includes managerial staff, guards, guides, and others. Hire necessary personnel. List who will be in charge of personnel, how long it will take to hire them, and how much it will cost.

- Decide what level of training in tourism management is necessary for all personnel. It will likely vary by position. Determine the best way to conduct training. Options include hiring a trainer to come on site, sending personnel to formal training programs, or sending personnel to visit another site with trained personnel. List what skills are needed for park personnel, who will be in charge of training personnel, what the best method of training is, how long it will take to hire them, and how much it will cost.

BRIDGES OUTSIDE PARK BOUNDARIES

The following considerations deal with interaction between the park and local communities.

- Having identified what communities will be impacted by tourism to the park in phase one, interaction with communities must continue. Interaction will depend on local cultural and socioeconomic conditions. For example, it may be appropriate to interact with elders in some places and the whole community in others. Set up individual meetings with each community to discuss their interest in tourism and what role they would like to play with tourism to the park. List what skills are necessary to work with communities, who will be in charge of community relations, how long it will take to make initial contacts, and how much it will cost.

- Select representatives from communities to participate in the tourism development plans and to be members of the ecotourism committee for the park.

- Provide assistance and support to communities that want more information about tourism to the park, have concerns about it, or want access to training or funding in order to participate in tourism development. List what skills are necessary to assist the community, who will be in charge of community relations, how much time this position will take, and how much it will cost.

- Hold regular meetings with communities to ensure that they are benefitting from tourism and minimizing its costs to their lifestyles. List who will be in charge of community relations, how much time this position will take, and how much it will cost.

The following considerations deal with regional (within the country) infrastructure.

- Decide what regional developments (roads, health clinics, accommodations, etc.) need to be built to support the park's proposed ecotourism plan.

- Lobby appropriate groups (government, private sector) to develop what is needed. It will be important to be able to articulate the benefits of ecotourism to the park for the whole region. List what skills are necessary to lobby groups, who will be in charge of this effort, how long it will take, and how much it will cost.

The consideration below has to do with other regional attractions.

- Decide if there are any other tourism attractions in the region that the park would like to coordinate with to create "regional" tourism packages. This would be part of promoting and marketing the park. Contact people from those attractions who would make good partners and make arrangements to do so. List what skills are necessary to work with other sites, who will be in charge of this marketing effort, how long it will take, and how much it will cost.

The following considerations take a national perspective, such as legal framework, policy considerations, and budgetary issues.

- Name the party (individual, agency, or consortium) that is officially in charge of tourism management in the park.

- Determine tourism zones for the park. Delineate these areas with official markers. List what skills are necessary to create zones, who will be in charge of zoning, how long it will take, and how much it will cost.

- Determine an entrance fee for the park. It may be best to have different fees for foreigners and nationals. Fees may include day rates, weekly rates, group rates, etc. Establish an entrance system to determine what physical structures and personnel are necessary. List the skills needed to develop an entrance fee system, who will be in charge of this activity (it may involve a national legal process), how long it will take to establish the system, and how much it will cost.

- Examine the national budgeting system for the parks. Is there a financial mechanism in place to bring entrance fee revenues back to the park? If not, begin the procedure to establish one. It may be useful to see how similar mechanisms have been set up in other countries. This may be a challenging procedure, but is critically important to the financial viability of the park. List what skills are needed to work on the financial system, who will take charge of this project, how long it will take, and how much it will cost.

- Determine budget allocations within the park itself. If tourism is a priority for the park, appropriate adequate funds for tourism development so that the park is prepared and can benefit from tourism. List the skills needed to handle budgeting, who will be in charge of the park budget, how long it will take to finalize, and how much it will cost.

These last considerations focus on how the various levels interact with the private sector.

- Decide which tour operators it is best to collaborate with. Decide what role the tour operators should play. (For example, should they bring their own guides or will the park supply guides?) List who will be in charge of handling tour operators, how much time this will take, and how much it will cost.

- Decide what information the park wants or needs about tourism demand. (For example, demographic information about visitors, what they like or do not like about the park.) Enlist tour operators as necessary to learn more about tourism demand. Conduct studies or surveys to fill in missing information. List the skills needed to research information, who will be in charge of tourism information, how much time this will take, and how much it will cost.

■ Decide how to promote and market the park. This may include developing a "visit the park" campaign, contacting travel writers to do stories, printing brochures, or leaving the whole issue to tour operators. Establish a marketing program. List the skills needed to promote the park, who will be in charge of promoting the park, how much time this will take, and how much it will cost.

PHASE THREE: WRITE AN ECOTOURISM STRATEGY DOCUMENT

Once a strategy is determined by the group, someone will need to be appointed to record the information, publish it, and distribute it. The ecotourism strategy can then be circulated to potential funding sources, donors, investors, or others who may offer technical assistance to the park management to actualize the strategy.

The ecotourism strategy will serve another function: it will become the official ecotourism plan for the area. Any development or tourism activity must follow the guidelines of the plan. Any changes to the document must be approved by the ecotourism committee for the park. The ecotourism strategy should be incorporated into the overall management plan for the protected area.

Given the importance of this document, it is critical that it be completed shortly after the workshop and that it is done professionally. For these reasons, it may be useful to hire a consultant for this phase, preferrably the same person from earlier phases.

METHODOLOGY

The methodology for the strategy document involves its preparation, publication, and distribution.

First of all, appoint someone to take the lead for phase three (the designee, a professional consultant). The designee will attend the workshop and record the results. At the end of the workshop, the designee will make a brief presentation of the results to the participants to make sure that the record is accurate. The designee will then write up the phase three report and circulate it to the ecotourism committee for review.

After receiving comments from reviewers, incorporate final changes from the ecotourism committee, and select a printer. Next decide on the format for the publication. Part of this process is identifying audiences for the report. Once audiences have been targeted, determine the number of copies necessary. Finally, seek funds for publication, if necessary.

Determine the best method of distribution, then seek funds for distribution, if necessary. Finally, circulate the report to all interested parties as well as potential donors and technical aids. Publicize the report as necessary.

CONCLUSION

Parks are becoming more and more interested in ecotourism. Not only are they receiving greater numbers of visitors each year, but park managers are starting to see tourism as a new source of funding and employment. But in order to get involved with ecotourism and keep the costs and benefits in balance, parks must be prepared for ecotourism. This set of guidelines is designed to help park managers in the planning process. It may be used as a thought piece for park managers who are confronting ecotourism and wondering what issues they face. Or it may be used as a guide for a formal planning process that will involve many people interested in ecotourism in the area and will result in an official ecotourism strategy for the park.

The important point is that the process described here is just a reference for the planning process. It should be used as a launching pad and modified as necessary to fit particular situations. The whole process of developing an ecotourism strategy will be individualized for each park. Therefore, this document is not an official recipe, just a starting point for putting a plan together. The key ingredient will be creativity on the part of the planners. Another crucial piece to making this process work is adequate financing. As mentioned earlier, most parks are facing enormous budget shortages. In order to create and implement an ecotourism plan, funding must be available for these activities. Hopefully, governments, conservationists, and the tourism industry will recognize the importance of ecotourism plans and support their development.

The purpose of this planning exercise is to ensure that protected areas are in a position of authority with ecotourism growth. Ecotourism will be a successful industry only if natural resources are protected. And natural resources will be best protected if there is a management strategy in place, and park managers and local communities take a lead role in the process.

Developing and Implementing Ecotourism Guidelines for Wildlands and Neighboring Communities

Sylvie Blangy and Megan Epler Wood

Ecotourism is defined as responsible travel to natural areas that conserves the environment and sustains the well-being of local people. This type of travel is dependent upon the conservation of wildland resources. A natural partnership exists, therefore, between the private enterprises that deliver nature-based travel experiences and the organizations (governmental, nongovernmental, and private) responsible for the protection of natural areas. Such a partnership can work to produce a genuine ecotourism experience by: raising public awareness of environmental protection, providing an economic resource for wildlands management, maximizing economic benefits for local communities, fostering cultural sensitivity, and minimizing the adverse effects of visitors on the natural and cultural environment.

Natural history tourism has always existed, but there has been a significant increase in this type of travel since 1980. In the 1980s many nature-based tour operators were experiencing over 20 percent growth in clients per year. Tourists are now found in increasing numbers in the most remote destinations on earth, from Antarctica to New Guinea. Wildland destinations are threatened by the rapid growth of tourism, and rural settlements surrounding popular destinations are often heavily affected by the invasion of foreign visitors. Local agencies responsible for visitor management can be greatly assisted if tour operators and environmental organizations inform visitors of appropriate behavior before they arrive in protected areas. The need to disseminate guidelines designed to protect fragile ecologic and cultural settings is now greater than ever.

Guidelines are a fundamental communications tool to reduce visitor impacts. They can be particularly useful before enforceable regulations governing visitor behavior are established. Ideally, all protected areas should have guidelines for visitors. However, there are many instances where local, state, and federal agencies are not generating any information for tourists. Private tour operations, environmental organizations, local communities, professional associations, and even airlines play an increasingly important role in educating visitors.

TYPES OF GUIDELINES

The objectives of ecotourism guidelines vary according to the entity formulating them. Objectives include helping visitors to: plan a trip and choose a tour, minimize impact when hiking and camping, and be a responsible traveler—environmentally, socially, and economically.

Most guidelines are targeted at visitors to natural areas, parks, and protected areas. The formulation of well-designed guidelines must take the many types of visitors into account. Similar to any other communications tool, guidelines need to be carefully targeted to the audience intended to benefit from them.

The visitor types listed below can be addressed either in a general set of guidelines or in a series designated for each group.

Visitors with tour groups	Boaters, snorklers, divers
Unescorted day-use visitors	Souvenir hunters
Unescorted overnight campers and backpackers	Bird watchers
Scientists	Bicyclists
Collectors	Off-road vehicle users
Amateur photographers	Cross country skiers
Professional photographers and filmmakers	Snowmobilers

Guidelines that address visitor services are also beneficial. Protected area managers are best suited to taking a leadership role in this category. If the protected area has a concession system, specific requirements can be defined and agreed to by contract before a tourist business is allowed to operate in the area. If there is no concession system, the management of tour operations, lodges and all other accommodations, and any other private enterprises surrounding the area, can best be prevented from creating a negative impact by providing guidelines that are as specific as possible.

Finally, guidelines targeted at the professionals involved in delivering information to visitors—tour guides, hospitality workers, information booth staff, shop employees—can best be developed by professional associations. Their role should be to upgrade services and protect the environment, thereby protecting the quality of life and work in the region.

PROCESS AND PARTNERS IN DEVELOPING GUIDELINES

Protected area managers seeking to attract tourists should consider *guidelines one of the most cost-effective visitor management tools available.* Providing guidelines is a genuine service for visitors who need and usually appreciate tips and information on how to behave. Much of the environmental and cultural damage caused by tourists is due to a lack of information and understanding. Simple and inexpensive information and outreach techniques can prevent irreversible damage to the region.

All the entities affected by visitors should be involved in the generation of guidelines. This can eliminate overlap and help make guidelines more comprehensive. It is best to survey what guidelines already exist and work with the organizations that generated them. For protected area managers, making guidelines part of a community involvement program is an effective way to ensure that local people are involved in and committed to their implementation. It also helps to prepare the community for the full range of tourist behaviors they are likely to encounter. There are several phases in the development of good visitor management guidelines. The nature and stage of development of the guidelines will help identify the appropriate partners to involve.

The first phase is the one in which principles must be established to lay the foundation for the formation of the guidelines. These principles provide the groundwork and help determine the objectives for the guidelines. For example, is the area a recreational area first, where resource protection is secondary or vice versa?

In the second phase, guidelines are developed after basic principles are agreed upon. Guidelines suggest appropriate behavior of visitors in a series of commonly occurring circumstances, such as the storage of food in campgrounds and how to dispose of all waste. "Pack out what is packed in" is a classic guideline. As guidelines develop they will become increasingly site-specific. Ultimately they will become the basis for regulations.

And in a final phase regulations can be developed from guidelines. However, they require adequate enforcement personnel and researchers that can make recommendations backed by field data on specific visitor impacts on soils, water, endangered species, and classes of habitat.

The following organizations all have a role to play in the creation of an effective system of guidelines.

Communities seeking to inform visitors of local customs can be most helpful with principles and guidelines relating to social morays and customs.

Private enterprises—outbound and inbound operators, private reserves, lodges, airlines, and equipment supply vendors—are all seeking to inform their customers. They often work well in partnership with not-for-profit environmental organizations to develop guidelines. These guidelines can be informative and useful to visitors in advance of their travels. The preparation of site-specific guidelines is best handled by protected area management in cooperation with tour operators. The input of tour operators can be very useful in sections outlining recommended procedures for controlling visitor group behavior in various habitats.

Not-for-profit environmental organizations may take the initiative and write guidelines if there are none available for fragile natural areas, as was done by Asociación Tsuli Tsuli/Audubon of Costa Rica. Or they can bring their expertise to bear by working cooperatively with both tour operators and protected area managers to develop a coordinated set of guidelines.

Tour guides and other interpretive workers may want to work together to set ecotourism standards, such as the code of conduct prepared by commercial operators and guides in the Queen Charlotte Islands in British Columbia, Canada. Guidelines generated by tour guides can be quite site-specific and provide useful background information on danger zones or sites where special care should be taken for the protection of endangered species. Tour guides who actually handle visitors on a day-to-day basis can be the most informed source of information for all phases of guideline development.

Many of the existing guidelines collected for this paper were created by state and national agencies in the United States (See Table 2-1). In addition, private tour operators are increasingly generating their own guidelines because of the lack of guidelines generated by developing countries. As tourism to developing countries continues to grow rapidly, responsible tour operators seem to be taking the lead. But they cannot do a sufficient job on their own.

Tour operators surveyed for this paper expressed great interest in guidelines generated by local land managers, regional agencies, nongovernmental organizations, and communities in developing countries. These entities are in a position to generate the most accurate set of standards for visitor behavior in their areas. Regulations with enforcement would be even more useful, but guidelines can be an important first step in lieu of regulations. Visitors need to be informed of the fragile habitats and species that call for particular caution in every natural area.

A sample set of guidelines incorporating all the information gathered for this chapter is found in Table 2-2 at the end of this chapter. These sample guidelines provide a useful reference point for the style and techniques described in the following sections of this chapter.

TECHNIQUES FOR GENERATING GUIDELINES

Here are some of the key points to consider when beginning to compile a set of guidelines.

- Decide who is the primary audience for the guidelines (e.g., general visitors, tour operators, user groups).

- Identify the theme or key thrust of the guidelines (e.g., environmental protection or increased cultural awareness).

- Consult with guides who lead tourists into target areas.

- Get technical assistance from scientists who have studied tourism's impact.

- Gather all the partners concerned around the table. Form a committee which may include residents, resource managers, guides, commercial operators, lodge owners, service personnel, and local vendors.

- Use guidelines from other areas as a model.

- Set objectives and formulate a way to evaluate whether the objectives have been met. (e.g., a decreased level of animal harassment or trail erosion).

- Work up the document and send it back and forth between the committee and technical specialists for review and criticism.

- Create a distribution plan for the guidelines document.

STYLE TIPS

Guidelines are written to solicit cooperation. They must be written with skill and insight into how the reader will interpret and use them. Write in a style that is friendly in tone. Avoid technical language that the reader may have to struggle to understand. If the guidelines are easy to read and written in a style that predisposes the traveler to cooperate, the time put into their preparation will pay for itself many times over. The following style tips are recommended.

- Be self-explanatory: explain why, use examples that illustrate consequences.

- Be positive: avoid language that prohibits actions. Encourage responsible behavior.

- Use figures and drawings to help explain consequences.

- Translate guidelines into as many tourist languages as possible.

- Print on recycled paper where feasible.

- Guidelines should be supplemented by tips on where and how to best view wildlife, safety recommendations, and a directory of contacts for more information. Requests for donations are also appropriate.

- The name, address, and phone number of the organization that prepared the guidelines should be clearly marked.

- A questionnaire for visitors on the effectiveness of guidelines should be considered.

POINTS FOR GUIDELINES REVIEW

Take into consideration the points (ecologic, social, and economic) listed below when drafting guidelines.

Ecologic guidelines are the backbone of a guidelines program, often designed by natural resource specialists experienced in the impacts of tourism on local ecosystems.

Garbage disposal	Feeding or touching animals
Human-waste treatment	Pet care
Firewood collection and fuel self-sufficiency	Protection of clean water supply
Campfire placement	Noise levels of campers, vehicles, radios
Campsite placement	Visual impact of visitors on other visitors
Trail, driving, or boating behavior	
Endangered species protection	Group size
Suitable distances for wildlife	Collecting natural souvenirs
Viewing and photography	Purchasing natural souvenirs
	International trade laws

Social guidelines are best generated by local communities. Failing that, the entity generating guidelines should seek extensive input from local leaders.

Local customs and traditions	Use and abuse of technological gadgetry
Religious beliefs	
Permission for photographs and other social favors	Bartering and bargaining
	Indigenous rights
Dress	Local officials
Language	Off-limits areas
Invasion of privacy	Alcoholic beverages
Response to begging	Smoking
Keeping promises	Tipping

Economic guidelines are an important component of social issues. As the field of ecotourism develops, ecotourists are being asked to recognize not only their impact on environments and culture but also on foreign economies. It is therefore important to consider integrating suggestions on the selection of goods and services that tourists purchase. In every instance the objective will be to reduce the leakage of revenue from tourism out of the region and provide for maximum revenues to local communities and protected areas. Because economic guidelines are a new concept, it may be necessary to explain in the guidelines how tourism revenues can provide a sustainable economic alternative to local people who might otherwise need to engage in unsustainable resource use to survive. Guidelines relating to the local economy include:

Purchasing local products

Paying user and entry fees

Making donations to local nonprofits

Using locally-owned restaurants and lodging

Appropriate tipping procedures

FUNDS AND SPONSORS

National and regional agencies can initiate guideline programs inexpensively by allocating staff time to the project. Public agencies can also encourage local groups to conceive and adopt their own guideline documents by allocating a small amount of funding to bring in a meeting facilitator, or to help with the design and editing of a brochure.

Outbound operators have expressed their willingness to help their local partners generate guidelines, including inbound operators, public land managers, and local communities. International and local nongovernmental organizations often have funds for environmental education projects. And tourist boards interested in promoting ecotourism should be asked to allocate funds for the generation, printing, and distribution of local guidelines.

IMPLEMENTING GUIDELINES

Guidelines for tourists are needed at a variety of different times during a vacation. Specific guidelines are the most appropriate when made available on-site. If the tourist can view the impact of tourism or see the fragility of the natural area being protected after reading the guidelines, it will make all the dos and don'ts more clear.

It is particularly effective to back up printed guidelines with a briefing. The ideal time to offer the briefing is right before departing for the day's field trip. Naturalist guides should be knowledgeable about tourism's impact. They should explain the guidelines, give examples of impacts they have observed, and ask for questions. During the field trip the guides should know when to say "no." In protected areas a policy banning payment to guides to get closer to wildlife should be established. A special fund for guides or guide training can be created by protected area management to relieve visitors of the pressure to give big tips to individual guides. A policy that offers tourists a way to give something extra to guides, without paying for bad behavior, is the model.

Much of tourism's impact can be caused by overchallenging visitors. For example, inexperienced swimmers, snorkeling for the first time, will stand on coral heads to adjust their masks or catch their breath. The consequences of inadvertent contact with fragile resources should be made known to visitors before they sign up for a trip. Areas that are not fragile should be reserved for visitors who need to learn how to avoid damaging the resource.

DISTRIBUTION

It is helpful to make guidelines available to visitors throughout a visit. Some possible outlets include:

Travel guidebooks

Hiking and road maps

Promotional brochures

Predeparture literature from
tour operators

Airline seat pockets

Rent-a-car desks

Visitor centers (hand-outs and
signs)

Park entrance literature, posters,
and signs

Guest rooms

Outfitter sales desks (e.g., scuba,
fishing, hiking, bicycling
services)

Visitors on an airline trip or in a visitor center could particularly benefit from a film or video backing up written guideline materials. Getting the message across visually will underline the consequences of bad behavior in a way that written materials simply cannot accomplish.

Publicity for new guidelines can help with the distribution process. International Expeditions, an outbound operator, announced their guidelines to the press via a formal media campaign. The campaign was targeted to international travelers and to travel agents. The guidelines have been enhanced in a press kit and incorporated into brochures. In certain instances television and radio announcements should also be considered. Distribution of posters and fliers at meetings with interest groups and the use of prewritten editorial pieces are also effective ways to get the message out.

It is important to have tourists routed through visitor centers or kiosks where guidelines are available. It will do little good if tourists do not see signs or literature with guidelines before entering a fragile natural area. This is a common problem. Protected area staff should make sure private bus drivers and guides direct their customers to information areas, and of course, make sure the information centers are well stocked with guideline information. Providing inexpensive guideline handouts to all private transport companies shuttling tourists through natural areas is another way to ensure tourists read guidelines before entering fragile sites.

EVALUATION

Little has been done to evaluate the effectiveness of guidelines. However, travelers can be surveyed on their return home and asked to share how well their trip complied with the published guidelines distributed.

If the objectives of the guidelines have been carefully defined and relate to specific sites or specific species, guideline effectiveness can be measured by assessing the relevant level of tourism impact on the target wildland or species. In the case of the "Save the Manatee" guidelines in Florida, the organizations that developed the guidelines documented that mortality and injury to manatees has dropped significantly since guidelines were distributed in conjunction with an extensive public relations campaign.

If a questionnaire is printed on the back of the guidelines, it can serve as an important consumer feedback mechanism. This feedback may be extremely valuable and bring out examples that could be incorporated into a revised document. Provide several well-posted receptacles for visitors to drop the questionnaires. Have park personnel ask for questionnaires as visitors exit. Provide a notebook for park staff to note verbal feedback from visitors as they exit. Using guidelines as a feedback mechanism may save on park maintenance by helping staff to catch trouble spots early. And questionnaires give visitors the rewarding opportunity to help with conservation controls.

TECHNICAL ASSISTANCE

Who is willing to provide technical assistance? The organizations below are good starting places.

The National Audubon Society has local chapters all over the United States and Central and South America. These local associations gather very knowledgeable scientists, amateur ornithologists and naturalists who can in many instances provide reliable information on tourism impact. Audubon has generated guidelines on both the national and local levels. The National Audubon Society can make copies of their "Travel Ethic" available.

Recreation Equipment, Inc. (REI) can make their "minimum impact guidelines" and "kid in the outdoors" brochures available in large quantity to any organization or person who wants to educate campers and back-country hikers.

Wildland Adventures has company guidelines that can be made available to other tour operators. In addition, Kurt Kutay, owner of Wildland Adventures, is involved in the preparation of industry guidelines (for nature tour operators in North America) on behalf of the Ecotourism Society.

International Institute for Peace through Tourism is conducting a questionnaire in order to draft a code of ethics for the larger travel industry.

The Ecotourism Society has guidelines on file for wildlands worldwide. Samples of all the guidelines listed on the following pages under "Recommended Guidelines" are available on request for the price of copying and postage. Research assistance on the guidelines applicable to specific areas or cases is available at extra cost.

U.S. Forest Service employs a "Leave no trace" coordinator. He is able to provide materials and answer questions regarding experience in minimum-impact camping and hiking in the U.S. National Forest System. Their program includes a large-scale training program in addition to written guidelines.

EXISTING GUIDELINES

Seventy sets of guidelines from all over the world were collected for this chapter. They were sorted by type of organization, target audience, topics, messages, and strategies. Six different types of organizations have developed ecotourism guidelines.

Religious and ecumenical groups, e.g., church councils

Tourism industry, e.g., tour operators

Environmental nongovernmental organizations

Governments, e.g., national and local land management agencies

Retail outdoor equipment vendors

Consumer associations

Religious and ecumenical organizations were the first to set up codes of ethics for tourists. Such guidelines were targeted at social ills such as child prostitution. This effort grew into larger programs that incorporate respect and concern for the natural environment in developing countries.

The nature-based tourism industry, commercial and nonprofit, have been pioneers in the field of environmental travel ethics. Their guidelines are aimed at natural history travelers offering common sense principles on how to behave in the wild.

U.S. state and federal agencies have informed and drawn visitor attention to endangered species protection programs. They have made an effort to convey a conservation message to travelers visiting public land. Enforcement and regulations with penalties are part of these programs.

Retailers, such as REI (Recreational Equipment, Inc.), have used their catalog and retail outlets to raise environmental awareness by distributing guidelines to their consumers.

Green consumer organizations—COOP AMERICA, for example—provide useful tips to subscribers on choosing an ecotour.

RECOMMENDED GUIDELINES

The following list provides a representative selection of well-written guidelines. All of these guidelines are available from the Ecotourism Society or directly from the organizations.

A Code of Ethics for Tourists (Ecumenical Coalition on Third World Tourism, c/o Center for Responsible Tourism, P.O. Box 827, San Anselmo, California 94979, Tel. 415-258-6594). The most popular and widely publicized and probably the first code of ethics to be developed. The code emphasizes social morays for travelers, such as bargaining ethics and appropriate dress.

Travel Ethic for Environmentally Responsible Travel (The National Audubon Society, Travel Program, 950 Third Avenue, New York, New York 10002, Tel. 212-546-9140). The most comprehensive guidelines addressing environmental, social, and economic issues. This document encourages travelers, tour operators, and guides to strengthen their efforts to support conservation in host countries.

Antarctica Tour Operator and Visitor Guidelines (Society Expeditions, Mountain Travel and Travel Dynamics, contact Society Expeditions, 3131 Elliot Avenue, Suite 700, Seattle, Washington 98121, Tel. 206-285-9400). Three tour operators developed two sets of guidelines based on the Antarctic Treaty. The visitor guidelines have been adopted by all of the U.S. ship tour operators. The tour operator guidelines propose better coordination to avoid overvisitation. Useful tips are offered to treat sewage and waste on board.

Gwaii Haanas Code of Conduct (Charlotte Husband, Box 733, Queen Charlotte City, British Columbia, V0T 1S0, Canada). Guidelines developed for and by commercial tour operators, resource guides, and visitors for protecting the Gwaii Haanas archipelago, also known as the South Moresby National Park Reserve. The guidelines represent a consensus document endorsed by operators as a code of conduct for commercial operations and visitors. This comprehensive set of guidelines includes tips on contact with archeological and cultural sites, the harvesting of fishes and shellfish, and the visitation of bird nesting areas. The guidelines also encourage the employment of local crews and guides.

Ecotravel Principles and Practices (Wildland Adventures, 3516 NE 155th Street, Seattle, Washington 98155, Tel. 206-365-0686). The ecotravel principles are the only guidelines to strictly apply a definition of ecotourism (the Ecotourism

Society definition). These guidelines cultivate an understanding and respect for the complex ecosystems to be visited and promote concern for the well-being of local people.

A Code of Environmental Ethics for Nature Travel (Asociación Tsuli Tsuli/ Audubon de Costa Rica, Apartado 4710-1000, San José, Costa Rica, Tel. 506-40-8775). A good example of guidelines adapted for a tropical country from the ethics published by the National Audubon Society.

Guidelines for Wildlife Viewing in Southeast Alaska (Alaska Department of Fish and Game, Division of Wildlife Conservation, Box 240020, Douglas, Alaska 99824, Tel. 907-465-4265). These guidelines focus on wildlife viewing in a cool coastal boreal habitat.

Guidelines for Protecting Manatees (Florida Department of Natural Resources, Save the Manatee Club, U.S. Fish and Wildlife Service, 100 Eighth Avenue SE, St. Petersburg, Florida 33701-5095, Tel. 813-896-8626). These guidelines help to protect an endangered species by advising on boat speeds, regulations for divers, and federal and state protection zones.

Code of Birding Ethics (National Audubon Society–Western Regional Office, 555 Audubon Place, Sacramento, California 95825, Tel. 916-481-5332). These guidelines offer excellent standards for birding enthusiasts, a highly specialized visitor type. They emphasize courtesy between birders, proper identification techniques, and photography ethics.

Plant Conservation Guidelines: Scientists and Teachers (Plant Conservation Roundtable, c/o World Wildlife Fund, 1250 24th Street NW, Washington, D.C. 20037, Tel. 202-293-4800). Especially designed for plant collectors, these guidelines give tips on how to assess the population before picking plants.

Ethics for Traveling Outdoorsmen and Researchers (Outdoor Ethics Guild, Bruce Banurski, General Delivery, Bucks Harbor, Maine 14618). Guidelines for collectors/researchers who need reminders to share data, work with local researchers, and provide final reports to host countries.

Leave No Trace Land Ethics (U.S. Forest Service, "Leave No Trace" Coordinator, Intermountain Region, Recreation and Lands, Federal Office Building, 324 25th Street, Ogden, Utah 84401, Tel. 801-625-5250). The most comprehensive guidelines on traveling through wilderness with a "no trace" land ethic. Unique pointers on planning wilderness trips and working with pack animals are included.

Minimum-Impact Camping: Techniques for the New Wilderness Ethic (Recreation Equipment, Inc., P.O. Box 88126, Seattle, Washington 98138, Tel. 206-395-3780). Attractive, well-designed, general guidelines for all outdoor enthusiasts.

Talamanca Guidelines (Talamanca Association for Ecotourism and Conservation [ATEC], Puerto Viejo de Talamanca, Limón, Costa Rica). Ecotourism pointers from a local community on the Caribbean coast. One of the few local groups to express their expectations from visitors.

Dance Etiquette (The Eight Northern Pueblos, Department of Tourism, 1100 St. Francis Drive, Santa Fe, New Mexico 87503). Social guidelines with pointers on photography, eating, dressing, collecting artifacts, village morays, and appropriate behavior at ceremonies.

Guidelines for Visitors to Mesa Country (Office of Public Relations, The Hopi Tribe, P.O. Box 123, Kykotsmovi, Arizona 86039). These guidelines were written after too many visitors imposed too much on Hopi hospitality. Visitors are reminded that they are guests and should respect the host's morays.

CONCLUSION

Guidelines are the most basic component of a complete, ecotourism management scheme. They should systematically appear in every highly visited site and accompany other visitor management policies, such as ongoing surveys of visitor traffic, nature interpretation, licensed guide services, zoning, and ranger patrols.

Because improving visitor behavior is so vital to meeting ecotourism objectives, public, private, nonprofit entities, associations, and local communities are all beginning to set their own standards. Setting professional standards and seeking the best ways to improve visitor behavior are excellent building blocks for the establishment of an ecotourism program.

It is important that local, national, and international organizations communicate and work together to establish guidelines. They should develop a base set of guidelines that is widely accepted for a diversity of sites and activities. These guidelines should apply to visitor behavior in a wide variety of circumstances. Once a master set of guidelines is complete, new more specific guidelines can still be formulated by participating resource groups.

Over-regulating tourist behavior should be avoided, but there are many ways to make guidelines more effective without spoiling the spirit of the visitor's holiday.

- Encourage pledges of cooperation, using guidelines as a "moral contract."

- Encourage resource-user associations (e.g., hiking or diving clubs) to adopt guidelines to help upgrade membership ethics and promote commitment to conservation.

- Use guidelines as part of environmental awareness campaigns to build more widespread comprehension of environmental travel and conservation ethics.

- Use guidelines as part of a curriculum for guide training programs.

- Use guidelines to help tourists evaluate the performance of their tour operator.

Creating guidelines for travelers is a fundamental building block of an ecotourism program. It is a positive and efficient way to encourage individuals to pay attention to their own behavior and contribute to conservation and sustainable tourism development worldwide.

Table 2-1. List of Ecotourism Guidelines Surveyed
(available from The Ecotourism Society)

Note: guideline title is given first, followed by the organization(s) that produced or published it.

Tour Operators, Business, Lodges

Gwaii Haanas Code of Conduct: group of resource guides, tour operators, and visitors

Antarctica Tour Operator Guidelines: Society Expeditions, Mountain Travel, Travel Dynamics

Code of Ethics: Oceanic Society Expeditions

Ecotravel Principles and Practices: Wildland Adventures

Fundamentals of Ecotourism: International Expeditions, Inc.

Suggested Traveler Environmental Guidelines: American Society of Travel Agents

Questionnaire for Ecotourism-Related Business: The New Keys, Costa Rica

Environmental and Cultural Travelers

Travel Ethic for Environmentally Responsible Travel: The National Audubon Society

A Guide for the Green Tourist: New England Governors' Conference, Inc.

Code of Eco-Tourism: Doug and Gail Cheeseman, Ecology Safaris, Inc.

Code of Ethics for Tourists: Ecumenical Coalition on Third World Tourism

How to Make Yourself Welcome in the South Pacific:
Justice in Tourism Network, New Zealand

Specific Sites, Settings

Antarctica Visitor Guidelines: Society Expeditions

Guidance for Visitors to the Antarctic: New Zealand Antarctic Research Programme

Antarctic Traveler's Code for Visitors and Tour Companies: Oceanites, USA

Oceans and Islands Visitors' Code: Salen Lindblad Cruising, USA

Guidelines for Wildlife Viewing in Southeast Alaska: Alaska Department of Fish and Game

Minimum Impact Code: Annapurna Conservation Area Project, Nepal

To All Hikers of the Inca Trail in the Historic Sanctuary of Machu Picchu:
Ministry of Culture, Tourism, Agriculture in Peru

Table 2-1. List of Ecotourism Guidelines Surveyed (Contd.)

Galápagos National Park Rules: Special Expeditions

Key Largo Reef Etiquette, and Keeping Your Keel Off Coral, Florida:
both from the National Oceanic and Atmospheric Administration (NOAA)

Desert Back-Country Ethics: Organ Pipe Cactus National Monument, Arizona

Recommendations for Travelers Visiting Natural Areas in Peru:
Fundación Peruana para la Conservación de la Naturaleza

Protect Our Coral Reefs: Reef Preservation Fund, Belize Audubon Society

Visitor's Guide to Antarctica: Turismo y Hoteles, Cabo de Hornos, Santiago, Chile

A Guide to Responsible Ecotourism:
Asociación Tsuli Tsuli (Audubon) de Costa Rica

Wildlife Watchers

Tips on Watching Wildlife: Colorado Division of Wildlife

Manatees (a guide for boating, diving and, snorkeling) and Guidelines for Protecting
Manatees: both available from Save the Manatee Club, Florida Power and Light Company, Florida Department of Natural Resources, and the U.S. Fish and Wildlife Service

Rules and Guidelines for Approaching Humpback Whales in Hawaiian Waters:
Sea Life Park Education Department, Hawaii

Guide for Viewing Wintering Bald Eagle: U.S. Forest Service,
Oregon Department of Fish and Wildlife, and the U.S. Bureau of Land Management

The Bears and You: Alaska Department of Fish and Game and the U.S. Forest Service

Encountering Marine Mammals in Alaska: Alaska Department of Fish and Game

Code of Birding Ethics—Good Rules for Wildlife Watchers: Sacramento Audubon
Society

Bird-Watching Etiquette—The Need for a Developing a Philosophy:
Richard J. Glinski and the National Audubon Society

The Ten Commandments of Birding Etiquette: Victor Emmanuel

Guidlines for Viewing Wildlife: Alaska Department of Fish and Game
and U.S. Forest Service

Table 2-1. List of Ecotourism Guidelines Surveyed (Contd.)

Specialists

Plant Conservation Guidelines: Scientists and Teachers:
Plant Conservation Committee, World Wildlife Fund

Ethics for Traveling Outdoorsmen (researchers) and Ethics for Traveling Outdoorsmen
(hunters and fishermen): both available from Bruce Bandurski, Outdoor Ethics Guild

The Scientific Codes of Ethics: Jean Colvin, University of California
Research Expedition Program

Campers, Hikers, Backpackers

"Leave No Trace" Land Ethics: U.S. Forest Service, National Park Service,
and Bureau of Land Management

Minimum-Impact Camping—Techniques for the New Wilderness Ethic:
Recreation Equipment, Inc. (REI)

The Wilderness Ethic, Back-Country Use: Rocky Mountain National Park, Colorado

Minimum Impact Techniques: Weiminuche Wilderness,
San Juan National Forest, Colorado

Hiking with Minimum Impact: Zion National Park, Utah

Minimum Impact Camping and Hiking: Crater Lake National Park, Oregon

Back-Country Etiquette, and Grizzly Country—Bear Us in Mind:
Yellowstone National Park, Wyoming

South Moresby/Gwaii Haanas Minimum Impact Camping: Canadian Park Service

Wilderness Camping, General Guidelines: The High Peaks Region

Planning and Choosing a Trip

Guidelines for Planning Travel/Study Experiences, Third World Travel—Buy Critically,
Suggestions for Responsible Travelers Taking a Cruise, and Responsible Traveling—
When Planning a Trip or Buying a Package Tour: all available from The Center for
Responsible Tourism

How to Support Responsible Tourism—The Ethical Traveler:
Co-op America, Travel Links

How "Green" is your Eco-Tour?: Michael Passoff, Earth Island Institute

What to Look for in an Eco-tourism Outfitter: Kurt Kutay, Wildland Adventures

Buyer Beware—Entry Refused: World Wildlife Fund, Division of Law Enforcement

Table 2-1. List of Ecotourism Guidelines Surveyed (Contd.)

Indigenous People, Cultural Events, Archeological Sites

Dance Etiquette, and Courteous Behavior When Visiting Our Pueblos:
Eight Pueblo Council, New Mexico

Guidelines for Visitors to Mesa Country: The Hopi Tribe, Arizona

Chaco Etiquette: Chaco Culture National Historical Park

What is Ecotourism?: Talamanca Association for Eco-Tourism and Conservation

Dos and Don'ts About Belizean Archeology: The Association for Belizean Archeology

Developers and Architects

Guidelines for Maya Participation in Ecotourism Planning and Development:
Betty B. Faust, Southern Oregon State College

Framework for Responsible Design for Ecotourism Facilities: David L. Andersen,
The Andersen Group Architects, Ltd.

Suggestions for Ecotourism Facilities and Small Scale Development Checklist:
Ecotourism Group of San Ignacio, Cayo District, Belize

Guidelines on Design and Construction for Sustainable Resort Development:
U.S. National Park Service

Guidelines for Ecotourism Facilities: Stanley Selengut, Maho Bay Camps, Inc.

Table 2-2. Model Guidelines for Tourists

The seventy guidelines reviewed offer the following tips for travelers.

Social Impact

Prepare well in advance of your trip. Take time beforehand to learn about the people and the place you are going to visit. Ask your travel agent or tour operator for detailed information about the destination country. Such information should be provided as soon as the trip is purchased. Go to the library for more information.

Allow plenty of time in each place. Spend sufficient time in an area to get to know and understand it. Avoid superficial visits. Make sure your schedule allows opportunities for meeting and interacting with local people. Try to stay at one site, rather than flying like a butterfly from one place to another.

Don't create barriers. Do not stay confined to your group. Mix with others. Use local transportation and services. Be receptive, ask questions, try to communicate in the native language. Look, listen, and learn from others.

Accept the differences, adopt the local customs. Culture, customs, religious sensitivity, lifestyles, and skills are different from your home country. Accept them, respect them, appreciate them. Try not to offend your hosts. Be culturally sensitive, especially when taking photographs, bargaining, and choosing your attire. Ask permission before photographing. Make sure your good deal is not robbery of the merchant.

Consider the effect of your visit. Do not make an extravagant display of wealth (for example, technological gadgetry). Beware especially of what you say and how you gesture. Do not leave your good manners at home. Do not encourage children to beg.

Be an ambassador back home. Share your experience with others. Maintain contact with the people you meet. Don't make promises that you cannot keep: send photos, for instance. Contribute to local projects and spread the word to fellow travelers.

Environmental Impact: For General Travelers

Make the right choice before you travel. Choose the right tour operators. Make sure they run their business with environmental sensitivity. When you plan to travel, find out about laws and regulations in the areas you plan to visit. Follow them. If you are an independent traveler, write or call for guidelines and contact the manager of the land you are visiting. Take the appropriate equipment with you.

Leave only footprints, pack it back, carry it in, carry it out. Do not leave anything behind: litter, trash, garbage, waste, disposal, leftover food, or even cigarette butts. Leave the site as clean as it was before human impact. Inquire about rules for proper disposal of human waste. Use designated areas, where possible, or bury waste well away from freshwater sources. Paper and organic matter can be burned if there is no danger of fire.

Table 2-2. Model Guidelines for Tourists (Contd.)

Be efficient with natural resources. Use energy, water, and other resources efficiently and in keeping with local practices. Participate in local recycling programs when they exist. Try biodegradable soap or detergent and use it well away from natural water sources. Gathering wood on the ground may be prohibited in dry or woodless areas. Portable stoves are recommended (stoves prevent fires). In general, be self-sufficient in fuel use. Do not deplete local resources.

Travel by your own muscle power. Go on foot, cycle, canoe, or use local public transportation, where possible.

Environmental Impact: For Hikers and Campers

Stay on the trail. Never take shortcuts. When traveling cross-country select your path and avoid stepping on vegetation. Overuse can lead to soil erosion or vegetation damage. This is particularly true for arctic tundra or arid desert, but it applies to most locales. Staying on the trail applies to vehicles, too. Cars, buses, jeeps, bikes, motorboats, canoes, and kayaks should stay within designated areas for transport, respecting speed limits and using charts that mark fragile zones, such as alpine vegetation, tundra, or coral reef areas. Drivers unfamiliar with specialized terrain should employ guides.

Low impact camping, staying overnight. Camp in a designated area. If no areas are specially designated for camping, camp away (100 meters) from water sources. Use existing campfire rings. On the beach, remove or scatter the ashes. Avoid crowding large groups into small camping areas. Keep groups small, ideally less than six people and no more than twelve. Speak softly, be aware of your impact on other users. Think of the noise disturbance. Leave pets at home or keep them leashed.

Environmental Impact: For Collectors

Take only pictures as souvenirs. Do not collect plants and animals or shells, corals, fossils, artifacts, stones, and eggs without permits.

Introducing plants and animals. Introduction of foreign plants and animals, whether intentional or accidental, can disrupt the ecologic balance of a region. Some countries are very concerned about introduced non-native plants. For example, New Zealand, Antarctica, and the Galápagos Islands are reducing imported organisms by thoroughly checking for nonindigenous species before passengers enter the territory. Check clothing, shoes, and camping equipment to avoid the accidental introduction of non-native flora and fauna.

Food gathering. Applicable size, catch limits and collection seasons must be observed. Be aware that national regulations may apply. In order to ensure preservation of stocks and resources, the commercial operators of the Queen Charlotte Islands (in the Gwaii Haanas Code of Conduct) have specified in their guidelines the local regulations for fishing and collecting shells and berries (rules include limit of catch, refraining from catch-and-release, maintenance of records, and possession of license).

Table 2-2. Model Guidelines for Tourists (Contd.)

Environmental Impact: For Wildlife Watchers and Photographers

Part of the experience for visitors is to observe wildlife. Learn appropriate stalking behavior and do not succumb to the urge to get too close. Photographers can be disruptive intruders in the wild. Use telephoto lenses—the longer the better—avoid flash photography with most mammals, and never bait animals with food.

Observe animals from the distance they consider safe; stay at a distance. All animals have "escape distances," that is, they'll let you approach within a certain distance before they try to escape. Observers should not violate this escape distance. Distances vary among species, individuals, and environmental circumstances and depend on the mode of transport. Here are some examples of distances submitted in the guidelines.

- Penguins, nesting birds, true seals: start with a baseline distance of 15 to 20 feet (5 meters).
- Walruses, otters, marsupials, plains herd animals: keep a minimum distance of 20 to 30 feet (8 meters).
- Manatees: 50 feet (16 meters) from an individual or a concentration.
- Fur seals: 50 to 60 feet (18 meters).
- Whales: not closer than about 300 feet (90 meters) and at a speed that matches theirs, approaching not directly from the front or rear, but parallel.
- Humpback whales: avoid an intentional approach within 100 yards (90 meters). If the craft is more than 100 feet long (30 meters), avoid within 1/4 miles (.40 kilometer). If cows or calves are present, stay beyond 300 yards (270 meters). By aircraft, stay beyond 1,000 feet (300 meters).
- Bears: as far as possible. Avoid encountering them, except at great distances. Observe with powerful binoculars or scopes.

How to approach and retreat. Approach wild animals slowly and quietly. Avoid sudden movements. Do not forget to retreat the same way you approached. You might have to crawl on the ground or walk with bent knees to get closer.

Learn the signs you are too close. Learn the wild animal behavior that indicates you are too close. The Alaska Department of Fish and Game has sketched the behavior of disturbed animals. Signs of fear, alarm, distress, aggression, and attack are described for birds, marine and land mammals, and fishes. In general, disturbed animals interrupt regular activities, such as feeding, start looking at observers, and take aggressive postures.

Learn the consequences of coming too close. If you come too close, remember you can be responsible for the loss or death of young animals. If nesting birds are flushed, chicks and eggs may die from excessive heat or cold, predators will eat unguarded eggs and chicks, and nests may be abandoned. Disturbance can cause animals unnecessary expenditure of energy.

Table 2-2. Model Guidelines for Tourists (Contd.)

Familiarize yourself with the local regulations. Always respect buffers and boundaries if they are indicated on a managed site. Do not go beyond these limits. Do not enter posted designated sanctuaries; these signs play a major role. The nautical charts in Florida, for instance, indicates to boaters and divers how to protect the manatees by observing speed signs and zones. If there are any local regulations or policies in the areas you are visiting, follow them.

Basic tips. Stay at the periphery of animal assemblages. Do not surround a group. Never get between animal parents and their young. Do not isolate one individual from its group. Give animals the right-of-way. Do not scare birds off nesting colonies. Do not attempt to touch animals. Follow these basic rules: keep your camp clean, store your food in a tree, camp well away from trails, and do not feed animals.

The should-nots. It is generally harmful, and often dangerous to: hand-feed, harass, chase, disturb, capture, or attempt to sell wild animals or the by-products of any living organism. Certain species are protected by law. The manatees, marine mammals, corals, flora and fauna of Antarctica and many other species are under protection of the Endangered Species Act or the Marine Mammal Act in the United States. The Convention of International Trade (CITES) has well documented lists of species prohibited in trade. Local regulations in each country visited must also be respected. Learn the rules for legal sales and purchase of animals and plants. See the "Buyers Beware" leaflet for trophies, meat, living organisms.

Returning home. Join environmental organizations. Become involved in conservation efforts. Pick up brochures and send money to local conservation projects. Keep in touch with your fellow travelers and let them know the latest on projects that are worthy of support. Give back, as much as you can, to the local authorities or to your hosts, in return for what you received.

Economic Impact

When choosing travel operators, ask these questions: How do they disburse their profits? Do they hire local guides and use local services and supplies?

When traveling, spend money on local enterprises. Choose traditional handicrafts and items made from renewable resources. Do not deprive people of rare and hard-to-get supplies. Do not encourage illegal trade by buying products made from endangered species. Shop around, but avoid bargaining with craftspeople to such a degree that their profits are only marginal.

ACKNOWLEDGMENTS

Organizations that provided information to this study appear below.

Co-op America, Travel-Links
2100 M Street, NW, Suite 310
Washington, D.C. 20063
Tel: 202-872-5307 or 800-424-2667

The Ecotourism Society
Carla Garrison
801 Devon Place
Alexandria, Virginia 22314
Tel: 703-549-8979

Department of Fish and Game
South East Alaska
Division of Wildlife Conservation
Marilyn Sigman
Box 240020
Douglas, Alaska 99824-0020
Tel: 907-465-4265

International Expeditions, Inc.
Tom Grasse
1 Environs Park
Helena, Alabama 35080
Tel: 205-428-1700

International Institute For Peace
   Through Tourism
Louis J. D'Amore
3680, rue de la Montagne,
Montreal, Quebec, Canada H3E 2A8
Tel: 514-281-9956

National Audubon Society, Inc.
Margaret Carnwright, Travel Programs
950 Third Avenue
New York, New York 10002
Tel: 212-546-9140

National Outdoor
   Leadership School
Bruce Hampton
P.O. Box AA
Lander, Wyoming 82520
Tel: 307-332-6973

Recreational Equipment, Inc.
Kathleen Beamer
P.O. Box 88126
Seattle, Washington 98138-0126
Tel: 206-395-3780

U.S. Forest Service
National "Leave no trace"
   Coordinator
William L. Thomson
Intermountain Region, Recreation
   and Lands
Federal Office Building
324 25th Street
Ogden, Utah 84401
Tel: 801-625-5250

Wildland Adventures
Kurt Kutay
3516 NE 155th
Seattle, Washington 98155
Tel: 206-365-0686

World Wildlife Fund
Ecotourism Program Officer
Elizabeth Boo
1250 Twenty-Fourth Street NW
Washington, D.C. 20037
Tel: 202-778-9624

The research for this chapter was made possible by Tod Nielsen who conceived and designed the project. Sylvie Blangy is grateful to him for hosting her at Discovery Tours of the American Museum of Natural History while she was on a leave from the Department of Agriculture in France. Megan Epler Wood would like to thank the Vermont Community Foundation for the unrestricted grant that made her work on this chapter possible.

Visitor Management: Lessons from Galápagos National Park

George N. Wallace

Galápagos National Park in Ecuador is not only a park but a world heritage site, a biosphere reserve, and now a marine reserve. Geologically, Galápagos is still forming via dramatic vulcanization and is the newest landform on earth. Isolated from the continents, the adaptations of its tortoises, iguanas, finches, giant cacti and sunflower cousins, flightless cormorants, pelagic birds, and many other flora and fauna are unrivaled in the world in what they tell us about our past and future. Galápagos may well be the best place on earth to study evolution at the ecosystem level. To experience the incredible marine, littoral, and terrestrial landscapes in which wildlife evolved with little or no fear of humans is truly unparalleled, not unlike being in the mythical garden of Eden. The archipelago consists of thirteen major islands, six smaller ones, and forty-two islets and rocks. Its land area covers almost 8,000 square kilometers (approximately 3,200 square miles) and the islands are spread over an interior sea of over 45,000 square kilometers (18,000 square miles).

Unlike many parks in Ecuador and elsewhere in Latin America, where people are legally and illegally found within protected area boundaries, people in Galápagos are not permitted to live in the park and are concentrated on the less than 4 percent of the Galápagos islands that is private land. Most visitors travel from the mainland by air to the islands of Santa Cruz or San Cristóbal. Tours then leave from the Baltra airport near Santa Cruz or the two main port towns near the airstrips where visitors arrive: Puerto Ayora (population approximately 6,000) on Santa Cruz or Puerto Baquerizo (population approximately 3,000) on San Cristóbal Island. Visitation sites are currently confined to a modest portion of the archipelago, so most of Galápagos is actually wilderness and has few visitors. Since the first commercial visits in 1969, there has been a slow steady increase in both services offered and the number of tourists coming to the Galápagos, as well as a large growth spurt after San Cristóbal was developed as a second arrival point and tourist support center. There were 7,000 visitors in 1975, 17,840 in 1985, and nearly 42,000 in 1989 (President's High Level

Commission, 1991). Interestingly, a 1973 park master plan called for a cap at 12,000 visitors and a 1981 Presidential Commission report called for a cap at 25,000 visitors.

During the first ten years of visitation, the park's initial management strategies and management assistance (from the Charles Darwin Foundation [CDF] which maintains a research station on Santa Cruz), worked relatively well with small numbers of visitors and continued to improve during the 1970s. Since then, regional economic woes and decreased Park Service budgets; increased pressures from the private sector; lack of political backing for park officials; and inadequate leadership, planning, and monitoring have combined with the increases in visitation to create concerns about the sustainability of park resources and management capability. Immigration and urban development continue at a rapid rate adjacent to the park and bring a whole new set of challenges. The introduction of exotic species continues to be a serious problem and concessions management leaves much to be desired. In addition, the quality of the experience provided to visitors is thought to be changing and is under study (Machlis et al., 1990; Wallace, 1991; Maldonado 1992).

In the Galápagos, the traditional tour is a one-week cruise on a boat to various visitor sites. In the mid-1980s national airfares became more reasonable and Galápagos experienced an influx of Ecuadorian visitors and a concurrent increase in the number of day-tour operators who take people out from the two port towns on short trips that better fit the budgets of Ecuadorian visitors in particular. Looking at all tours, there are now approximately six yachts, four ships (thirty-four- to ninety-passenger), seventy-five launches (eight- to sixteen-passenger), and ten sailboats. These are generally lucrative enterprises and the demand for permits to operate is great. In the last ten years, the process for the issuance of permits to operate a commercial tour boat has been controversial, highly politicized, full of loopholes, and once removed from those actually managing the park. Park defenders have long claimed that the park's carrying capacity was being exceeded and that no more permits should be issued. Investors wanting permits have countered that there was not proof of overvisitation and then asked various politicians to intervene on their behalf. In spite of the recent availability of techniques for judging and managing visitor impact, such as "Limits of Acceptable Change" (Stankey et al., 1985) and "Visitor Impact Management" (Graefe, Kuss, and Vaske, 1990), the focus in Galápagos in the past ten years has been on trying to arrive at some limits on the acceptable number of visitors. Such estimates of carrying capacity have been widely debated and poorly defended (Moore, 1992).

To complicate matters, tour boat permits, or "cupos" as they are called, have been administered by a much-abused two part process requiring the applicant to first get permission to navigate from the Merchant Marine (DIGMER) and later to finalize permission to operate with the Ministry of Agriculture (MAG), of which the Park Service is a part, but seldom with input from park managers. To make matters even worse, investors would use the merchant marine permit to obtain a loan to build a tour boat and then use the argument (often with politicians intervening) that their investment would result in economic hardship if the MAG "patente" or permit to operate were not granted. Nearly all such claimants have been given permits.

Even though the National Park Service in Galápagos (SPNG) has more resources than other parks in Ecuador, those resources are still very modest and put limits on staff, training, equipment, and infrastructure. Money generated from a $40 entrance fee paid by foreign visitors to the Galápagos, as well as fees paid by Ecuadorean nationals and tour operators, helps to finance other protected areas in Ecuador. The park's future is tied to the adjacent port towns that will require considerable investment themselves. As mentioned, these towns have grown rapidly with the increase in permitted tour operators. Puerto Ayora and Puerto Baquerizo are not able to provide adequate potable water, treatment of solid or liquid wastes, medical services, land use planning, port facilities for loading and unloading fuel and cargo, or other services that are needed to protect local residents, park visitors, and park resources.

In recent years Galápagos has been seen by many on the mainland as Ecuador's "mina de oro," or goldfield, thus attracting many boomtown immigrants. Prior to this, the native population in Galápagos was very small. The increase in population and the distance from the mainland has put tremendous pressure on the exploitation of park material resources such as fill dirt, sand, stone, and lumber. The fishery resources, once used mostly for local consumption, have been under heavy pressure to satisfy both national and international markets. Previously unharvested resources (sharks and sea cucumbers) have recently been severely exploited by Japanese fishermen for export to Taiwan. Nearly uncontrolled lobster fishing has been driven by the demand for export to Miami.

Although the 1980s and early 1990s have raised disturbing questions, the park is by no means in dire straits. Modifications and improvements are underway and many institutions are assisting to strengthen this great world park. In 1991, the president of Ecuador declared a (second) moratorium on the issuance of additional permits for commercial operators who wish to provide boat tours, and he formed a special multisectoral commission to come up with a plan for ecotourism and conservation for Galápagos. This author served as an advisor to that commission's technical committee. Since that time, the United Nations Development Program has provided considerable support to the commission, and the World Bank, through their joint program with the Global Environmental Facility (GEF), has expressed an interest in funding part of the actions proposed by the commission; proposals are being prepared (MacFarland et al., 1991). The next few years should see the implementation of improved coordination between the entities involved. Improved on-the-ground management has already begun.

Although this chapter precedes the conclusion of our current research in Galápagos, it draws on the author's relationship with park and Charles Darwin

Foundation staff over several years and takes a "lessons learned" approach that is generally optimistic.

Past and Current Visitor and Concessions Management

Several notable features have characterized visitor management in Galápagos National Park. First, the Park Service, with help from the Charles Darwin Foundation (the most important nongovernmental organization in Galápagos), has trained and certified commercial tour guides, and these guides are supposed to accompany all tours. Since visitors travel largely by boat, and eat and sleep on board, the need for significant infrastructure on outlying islands has been greatly reduced. Though a number of impacts are reduced on land, the system admittedly creates others in bays or harbors. Visitation sites typically have short, well-marked trails and visitors are asked to stay on the trail. These management features have been relatively successful at controlling many "biophysical" impacts at the approximately fifty-nine official visitation sites. Additionally, some islands that do not have exotic species are totally off limits to tour boats. It should be noted that some park users are not tourists at all but descendants of early immigrants (a mixture of agricultural pioneers, convicts, and other adventurers arriving after 1832) who have been long-term residents in Galápagos. Scientists have also used Galápagos for some time and have been influential in the establishment of the park and in shaping many management policies and activities.

The results of using guides and concessionaires as visitor-managers are mixed. In one sense it is innovative and reduces part of the need for visitor management infrastructure (interpretive programs, signage, permits, educational materials, and such). On the other hand, the tendency in recent years has been to reduce the Park Service's overall presence and it now appears to outside visitors to be relatively weak. Although patrols were common in the 1970s, some guides and boat captains comment that they did not see a park ranger out on patrol in the outlying portions of the park in the five years between 1986 and 1991. Priorities have changed and the park has had neither the staff, boats, nor fuel to do much patrolling. Other than fee collection at the airport and provision of assistance to the Charles Darwin Research Station at their visitor center and tortoise and iguana breeding units, on-the-ground visitor contact or visitor management activities by park rangers in the park itself have been limited.

On the islands of Santa Cruz, San Cristóbal, Floreana, and Isabela, where there is the potential for a number of land-based activities typical of other national parks, there are few visitation areas managed directly by the Park Service. By visitation areas we mean park-managed visitor centers, camping, picnicking, or hiking areas, interpretive or educational sites, the presence of working trail crews, or other visitor management activities. Moreover, there has been a noticeable absence of interaction with visitors by those rangers who are on patrol and visible in the park. The Charles Darwin Research Station does have a visitor center and interpretive activities outside the park where Park Service personnel are periodically present.

Because of the increase in permits granted, commercial tour activities are now so numerous and have generated such a large array of support services in the port towns that the private sector, in spite of its dependence on the park for its very existence, has taken on a life of its own. Tourism activities are out of balance with park and marine reserve management capability. Because of the rapid growth, overwhelming presence, diversity, monetary resources, and political momentum of the private sector, it is now much more difficult for park managers (who do not have an equivalent presence) to plan or implement decisions about site quotas, group size, acceptable levels of impact, zoning, tour scheduling, guide training, and other aspects of visitor and concessions management.

Though park rangers and administrators are of good quality in Galápagos, training is needed, pay is much lower than that offered in the private sector, and turnover is high. Many park staff members have commented to this author that they do not feel "in charge" of the park or what is happening in nearby communities. Among the complicating factors are the large size of the park, a lack of cooperation between agencies that have an odd arrangement of jurisdictions and responsibilities, limited time and resources, and the frustration about being unable to control increases in visitation until the corresponding park management capability is in place. Specific management concerns are outlined below.

SOME CURRENT PROBLEMS

Boat and equipment inspections are inadequate and some operators are not meeting specifications for visitor health and safety. Day-tour operations are especially problematic in this regard. The responsibility for such inspections falls to the Navy and the Ecuadorian Tourism Commission (CETUR) and should be shared with park officials. There are feelings on the part of those concessionaires who have high standards that the Park Service should begin jointly enforcing such regulations with the other agencies to prevent a decline in the quality of services.

Introduced species are a constant threat to Galápagos, especially the uninhabited islands, but also to the inhabited islands that already have many aggressive exotic species that are capable of out-competing the highly unique endemic species of Galápagos which evolved with few such threats. There are virtually no quarantine procedures or facilities for arriving goods, nor inspection of arriving passengers. Much of the Park Service budget is spent trying to control exotic species such as rats, pigs, goats, cats, and a variety of plants. There is also a reintroduction program for threatened species in locations where exotics have been controlled.

The system of training, rating, and paying guides has created a schism between "naturalist" guides (who are usually from the mainland or other countries, and who are better educated and better paid) and the "auxiliary" guides (who have less education, lower pay, and tend to be local). The system has become controversial, politicized, and hard to manage. Political pressure has developed to hire local guides and to put less emphasis on their interpretive skills, linguistic qualifications, or their understanding of park management principles. There is an unproductive tension among guides themselves.

The park's management plan and specifically its zoning and visitor management strategy is no longer adequate for the current level of visitation. It must be updated and even then it will be difficult to implement changes without the active participation of tour operators and other agencies (Cifuentes, 1992).

Before the era of increased permits and day tours, many early concessionaires (75 percent) developed *fixed itineraries that made coordination of site visits possible* and helped reduce crowding. The Park Service has not required fixed itineraries of the many new tour operators that now operate. The result has been that the eight to ten most popular sites near the port towns are experiencing congestion and a corresponding decrease in the quality of the visitor and operator experience along with suspected increases in biophysical impacts. Other sites, usually located further away from the port towns, may be underutilized. Itineraries and/or zone assignments must be more equitably utilized in the future.

New visitation sites—especially land-based sites in the interior of the larger islands that already have extensive complements of introduced species (Santa Cruz, San Cristóbal, Floreana, and southern Isabela)—can be developed to increase the supply of sites beyond those traditionally used by concessionaires. Until recently, the Park Service has found itself "out of the habit" of designing, building, and managing visitation areas and doing the low impact education that could accommodate some of the increase in visitors who arrive without a tour booking and choose to take day trips, or visitors who combine independent and commercial activities (26 percent, Machlis et al., 1990). A limited number of interior sites on the northern volcanos of Isabela and Cerro Azul and perhaps on Santiago could slowly be made accessible to small, specially permitted, and guided groups who are required to use only the strictest of practices in order to preclude the introduction or transferral of exotic species.

Compared to the visitor experience in U.S. or Canadian national parks, attraction site visits in Galápagos are, with some necessity, more homogenous and found in what are called "intensive use zones," *which do not often allow groups to linger or experience sites in a more leisurely way* or which minimize encounters with other groups. Furthermore, during peak visitation periods, visits can seem hurried (Wallace, 1991). The current zoning in the park is sensitive to resource constraints and has placed limits on visitation to ecologically pristine islands. It also includes "intensive and extensive" use zones, but has never deliberately been managed for a broader spectrum of visitor opportunities (distinct settings and experiences ranging from developed/intensive to primitive/low density) like those used in many parts of the world. Because of worries about species introductions, the "freedom to roam" will never be great, but refinements in the zoning system are due, as are management objectives that correspond to each zone.

Before the increases in visitation and number of tour boat operators, zoning inadequacies did not much matter because tours could periodically find some sites without other visitors and spend more quality time there. Now that the most popular sites provide the same kind of visitor experience, it will be important to design management systems with management objectives (such as site quotas and site-specific standards that purposefully separate intensive and more pristine experiences for some of these sites). It will also be important to zone and manage sites that are used frequently by local people and visitors where the emphasis is on recreation rather than on seeing and understanding the park's biotic or abiotic resources.

Many people who arrive to work in the Galápagos don't understand the unique and "world heritage value" of the park and their combined actions have an impact on the delicate environment. This even includes crew members aboard tour boats. The Park Service has not been funded, staffed or, until recently, prepared to take on the new but important role of outreach and education with local people. The limited presence of rangers out and about on patrol in areas near the towns complicates this. But the fact that park staff members also live in these same communities offers the potential for improvement once this becomes a priority.

More national visitors have been coming to the Galápagos in past years. The airfare for Ecuadorians has been up to 75 percent less than that paid by foreigners. Observers detect a difference in motivations, since some nationals come with the idea that Galápagos offers a typical beach holiday atmosphere rather than ecotourism or nature-oriented tourism. Among those interested in nature, the affordable day tours often chosen by Ecuadorians offer possibilities for understanding park ecosystems, flora, and fauna that are much more limited than the tours taken by those with more money. There is little Park Service input on, or control over, the national advertising images about Galápagos that forms visitor expectations. Though a study is currently underway to probe the motivations, expectations, and experience preferences of visitors to the Galápagos (Wallace and Wurz, 1992), foreign visitors, with many available beaches elsewhere, are thought to come to Galápagos predominantly for nature tourism while Ecuadoreans may come for a wider variety of reasons.

REASONS FOR OPTIMISM

As mentioned, the President's Commission and its Technical Committee, the Charles Darwin Foundation, and the Park Service itself have prompted activities to improve the situation in Galápagos. A variety of international and national organizations seem interested and willing to help sponsor needed improvements given the world importance of the park. Nongovernmental organizations continue to put considerable effort and resources into Galápagos, and there are a number of concessionaires who have already indicated a willingness to make needed changes.

There has also been a leveling off and slight decline in visitation during the past four years, which should give managers and concessionaires time to make improvements. This is likely a result of the regional outbreak of cholera, inclement weather, political unrest in neighboring countries (Peru and Colombia), and other problems in the region (reflected in warnings to travelers from the U.S. State Department), rather than any general dissatisfaction of visitors. For the most part, Galápagos is such a unique and marvelous experience that most visitors will put up with a lot of suboptimal experiences and outcomes and still report satisfaction with their trip (that is, until questioned in depth, at which time they will make suggestions about improving the quality of the experience [Machlis, Costa, and Cardenas, 1991]). Additionally, a trip to Galápagos is an expensive and logistically complex, once-in-a-lifetime experience for most foreign visitors. Researchers describe this as the perfect situation for rationalizing about one's experience ("Of course I had a good time after all that time, effort, and money; and after all, it is Galápagos"). In short, it still takes a lot to have a bad time in Galápagos, and the visitor mood is still positive despite many problems.

Studies will soon be complete that will assist in refining zoning and visitor management strategies, work already begun by the technical committee. A number of suggestions have emerged from the President's Commission that call for, and will support, permanent coordination between organizations such as the Park Service, the planning and development agency (INGALA), the Port Captain and Merchant Marine (DIGMER), the national tourism agency (CETUR), the Darwin Station, and others.

PRACTICAL LESSONS LEARNED

The remainder of the chapter will examine past and current visitor management practices, specifically current problems, and then focus on the solutions that seem to be evolving out of the work of many people concerned about this great park. There are many portions of the Galápagos story that will be relevant for the management of visitors and ecotourism concessions at other protected natural area destinations. Perhaps the most obvious lesson in all this is that increases in visitation to a protected ecotourism site or area should not be allowed to exceed the management capability to handle such visits, be they commercial or private. There is an ideal symbiotic relationship between concessionaires and protected area managers that is frequently out of balance in Galápagos and elsewhere. Managers need concessionaires to transport, help educate, and meet the needs of visitors in a geographically extensive archipelago-based park like Galápagos. Concessionaires depend on managers to insure that the resources people are coming to see are managed in a sustainable way and that the quality of the visitor experience is maintained. Ideally, managers provide the trails, visitor centers, patrols, inspections, interpretive materials, zoning, control of exotics, and the rest which ensure that concessionaires will have a good "product" to offer.

In developing countries such as Ecuador, concessionaires must invest in protected area management as part of the cost of doing business. Ecotourists who see this investment and concessionaire collaboration with management will, we think, pay for the experience willingly (Wallace, 1992; Cronin, 1990; Durst, 1988). Strong, well-managed parks and protected natural areas will always be marketable commodities providing benefits to the private and public sectors. Concessionaires must also remember that protected area managers must manage for more than the recreational and economic value of an area. They have important responsibilities to protect scientific, life support, biodiversity, historical, cultural, spiritual, and other values as well. Protected area managers in developing countries, where many areas are newly designated, are often understandably reluctant to allow as much visitation as they might due to their fear of impact on area resources and lack of confidence about managing visitors. Overly protective managers, reluctant to allow concessionaires to operate, must remember that ultimately, protected areas will not survive without constituents who know and love those places. Visitors/constituents are the ones who will drive the politics of conservation that provide the manpower and budgets for management of such areas, and who make the donations to nongovernmental organizations such as World Wildlife Fund, the Nature Conservancy, the Charles Darwin Foundation, and many others who in turn invest in protected area management. A balance must be struck.

PERMITS

In keeping with the above, ideally, there should be a distinction in all areas between a license to operate as a concessionaire (a business' professional and material ability to provide quality tours of a specific type: marine tours, river running, diving, pack trips, or lodging) and a permit to operate in a given area. Each area has its special set of criteria that determines whether or not a concession permit will enhance the manager's job or make it more difficult. In developing countries it may be necessary to combine licenses and permits at first, but only if local managers familiar with site-specific requirements have the final say. If this system is clear, then investors will recognize that they must have the full permit before proceeding with any investment. Owning a boat is not proof of suitability. Once the agency is satisfied that an operator will indeed help with the objectives of the park or protected area, then the agency "concedes" the privilege to operate a business enabling it to make a profit using public resources that belong to all. Many forget that this is indeed a privilege and not a right. Soils, terrain, climate, the needs of local people, visitor motivations and preferred experiences, the desired mix of visitor types, park resource management objectives, sensitive areas—these and other things which determine the conditions of a permit to operate, are known best by area managers and concessionaires and less well by those in the capital city unfamiliar with a protected area.

If one day a separate licensing process can insure that more general and less site-specific standards for training, equipment, insurance, bonds, a company's solvency, and other prerequisites for operating are in place quite apart from a particular ecotourism site, this will justifiably remove part of the burden from area managers. Professional associations have a legitimate role in helping to establish the standards for licensing and should be included on the boards that do so. In Galápagos, a recent decision has been made to form a unified commission so that the Ministry of Agriculture, the Park Service, the national tourism agency, the Merchant Marine, and commercial associations can monitor licensing procedures, but Galápagos National Park itself will have much more to say about the issuance of permits to operate in the park. Again, the essential lesson learned is that in the realm of concessions management, area managers must have ultimate control over permit issuance.

PRESENCE OF PARK PERSONNEL

Studies have shown that the presence of park rangers in uniform at entrances, on patrol, staffing visitor centers, aboard tour boats, interpreting, and visibly managing park resources has a positive impact on visitors (Manning, 1986). The presence of a public employee defines the place as belonging to everyone and lends a feeling of stewardship—that things are being looked after and will be there for one's children. A combination of park staff and volunteers, nongovernmental organizations, and concessions personnel is even better because it implies a joint effort. The presence of private sector representatives alone does not provide the same effect.

It is common knowledge that rules without enforcement can lead to disrespect and anarchy among visitors and concessionaires. The illegal extraction of sand and compromises to visitor safety in Galápagos are good examples of rules that are not sufficiently enforced. Only with park officials on patrol or otherwise present is there really an air of institutional and legal jurisdiction over management activities. Much of this feeling is still missing in Galápagos.

The fact that visitors are received at the airport by neatly uniformed park guards who collect fees is positive, but the opportunity to give an orientation talk on the airplane with an official welcome, or to talk about the severe problem of the introduction of exotic species, is being foregone. The image of guard as steward, authority figure, and source of knowledge is replaced by that of the ranger as ticket taker. In years past park rangers were in fact assigned to accompany cruise ships and interact more with visitors. Some problems surfaced at that time which must be addressed if park "presence" is to become more visible.

Because of the fact that many visitors do not speak Spanish and many park rangers do not speak English or French, special measures may have to be taken. First, those training to become commercial guides (usually bilingual) could be required to serve a six-month internship at the park where they would accompany protected area staff and thereby learn more about park management while serving as interpreter and language role models (MacFarland, 1992). The use of students and volunteers in such a role has much potential and has become common in other countries. Second, it should be the responsibility of all guides to respect and interpret group contact with park guards and continue the role played during the internship. Bilingual group members should be encouraged to interpret for the group when a bilingual guide is not present. Third, all park staff should have training in interpretation and in handling a variety of situations involving visitors. Visitor contacts should be encouraged. Fourth, in addition to informal contacts, the number of scheduled activities where park guards serve as information givers or interpreters should be increased. This can be accomplished via roving rangers or assignments pairing rangers with commercial guides to share the educational function. Rangers may be especially useful on larger boats if concessionaires are asked to carry out activities in smaller dispersed groups to conform to new zoning standards. Fortunately, such a return to "presence" should not be difficult since visitors frequently approach uniformed rangers for information.

Patrols are an essential part of park presence and the administrative life of a protected area. Park staff must know what goes on in all parts of an area—both remote and heavily used areas. Patrol schedules should be both random and scheduled for enforcement to be effective. Good concessions management with the rules fairly applied to all requires a strong field presence and a collaborative relationship with tour operators. This is seldom enhanced by leaving tour operators to operate alone or allowing some to take liberties with the rules while others do their best to observe them. Concessionaires in the Galápagos have indicated a willingness to invite rangers to accompany tours and are supportive of increased patrolling and monitoring of permit specifications. This is a relationship that is much easier to establish at the beginning, while operating in a protected area is still seen as a privilege, than to do it retroactively. The new park superintendent in Galápagos has made patrolling a priority. He has acquired some of the necessary patrol boats, radios, and other equipment, and developed a new strategy for patrolling and redistributing guard assignments throughout the archipelago (Izurieta, 1992).

Balancing Commercial and Noncommercial Opportunities for Visitors

There should be some access and activities provided by concessionaires and some provided to visitors by a protected area directly. There should never be a private sector monopoly on the movement of visitors. It is this author's opinion that, in order to maintain a management balance, few parks should have more than 50 percent of their activities commercialized. The need for outfitters/guides is more apparent in a park like Galápagos, which is more than 240 miles (400 kilometers) wide and where travel is by boat between island sites and where fragile ecosystems threatened by exotic species do not allow the freedom of movement by private parties that would be appropriate in many parks. Even in Galápagos, however, there is considerable potential to develop opportunities for visitors to hike, camp, swim, and dive in less fragile areas managed by the park (the interior portions and a few beaches on the inhabited islands of Santa Cruz, San Cristóbal, Floreana, and parts of Isabela where threats to pristine ecosystems are less of an issue).

There are also opportunities in the above mentioned areas to encourage the development of small local concessions on private land adjacent to lands managed by the park that would diversify the commercial offering in favor of local people and reduce some of the pressures from agriculture currently felt by the park. Both park-managed and local opportunities would be welcome alternatives providing balance to the now prevalent package tour. Such options would not only reduce costs for national visitors but also create a greater diversity of experience opportunities to choose from for all visitors. It is the development of some park-managed visitation sites that insures the aforementioned presence of rangers as managers and which can take a good deal of pressure off increasingly congested boat tour visitation sites.

For this to happen will require an increase in training that covers visitor management techniques (e.g., infrastructure design, use limits, site hardening and maintenance, visitor information, signage, monitoring, and patrolling). Since impact on park resources is often determined by the types of visitors present and their behavior rather than the number of visitors, visitor education that promotes behavior meant to reduce impacts is an essential and an important part of what is meant by "management capability." Unlike commercial tours where group size must be large enough to be economically viable, park-managed areas can serve smaller groups who wish to pursue activities that are more self-directed and provide an intimate experience like that provided by some of the smaller boats that visit outlying and less popular sites. Visitor centers and interpretive sites developed and staffed by the park are also important ways to provide noncommercial opportunities. Self-guided, volunteer, or ranger guided nature trails; campfire or meeting areas for speaking to groups of school children, local people, or visitors; and picnic areas sited and designed for use by local people are also important examples of ways to balance the public and commercial offerings.

It should be noted that as new and alternative sites are identified for management by the park, commercial tours should still be able to utilize such areas, providing the groups they bring are of appropriate size and are interested in utilizing low impact techniques. Pilot areas that introduce opportunities for limited hiking and camping could be utilized by unguided individuals or small groups that have received an orientation from park officials or by less experienced visitors who are accompanied by a guide. One recreational beach has become very popular with national visitors and island residents who seek recreation opportunities that do not involve more extensive trips into the park. The careful development of such developed and hardened recreation areas near the island communities is a way of enticing residents to take a closer look at other attractions the park has to offer, and will give them areas within the park where they feel comfortable in spite of not being tourists. Intensive use recreation areas also provide an opportunity for residents to mix with foreign visitors and guided tours in a nonbusiness leisure setting.

Additionally, the Park will soon encourage private landowners to develop recreation sites where either guided or unguided visitors arrive on their own, and which will be included as part of an overall management strategy to better distribute use. Along with the emphasis on park-managed areas, the staff is being sent, under the sponsorship of UNESCO and the Darwin Station, to study in areas where the art of in-park visitor management has had more time to evolve.

ZONING THAT HELPS MANAGERS AND CONCESSIONAIRES, AND IMPROVES THE VISITOR EXPERIENCE

It is a given that protected area managers need to find constituents (tourists, scientists, educators, local residents) who know and love the area that they manage. It is the long-term support from such people that will ensure the politics and budgets necessary to manage. A lesson being learned in Galápagos, as well as many other places attempting to improve visitor management, is that zoning should be done both to protect resources and to provide diversity in the experiences available to visitors. Likewise, monitoring should look at impact (positive and negative) both on the biophysical environment and on the experience of the visitor (Driver et al., 1987; Graefe et al., 1990; Stankey et al., 1985).

In addition to the legislation designating a protected area, the selection of management objectives for any unit within such an area is driven in large part by two things: resource constraints that are biophysical in nature such as soil type, altitude, precipitation, unique landscape or ecosystem features, the needs of wildlife or other such determinants; and by the availability, type, location, and distribution of desired experience opportunities for visitors: seeing wildlife of a certain type, or diving on a coral reef to see and easily understand an area's geology. These imply some combination of understanding what motivates people to come to a place, the outcomes they seek, and what is possible for managers to provide while protecting area resources.

Once different types of management objectives have been determined as appropriate for a given portion of a protected area, zones should be established and managed for distinct *setting attributes* that correspond to those management objectives. These setting attributes in a given zone can be described in terms of what is desirable: visitor density, number of encounters between visitors, amount of evidence of human activity and infrastructure, remoteness, type of travel, appropriate equipment, level of regulation or visitor freedom, all of which correspond to the necessary level of resource protection given an area's biophysical constraints. Researchers have found that certain visitor motivations can be paired with particular setting attributes producing a high chance of visitor satisfaction. Setting attributes should be distinct and have their own integrity in each zone in order to accommodate the diversity of visitor motivations that such studies almost always reveal (Driver and Brown, 1975, 1978). Where zoning systems are weak, setting attributes blend together as a result of management objectives not being well defined.

Galápagos has had *intensive use, extensive use,* and *scientific use* (off limits to all but a few visitors) zones for a number of years. At popular sites in the intensive zone, the normal experience opportunity is a two- to three-hour tour led by a guide, where encounters with other groups—both large and small boats—are the norm and preclude extended site visits. Recreation areas near the port fall within the intensive use zone, but may ideally have management objectives and setting attributes that differ from other visitor sites also zoned as intensive use. Areas zoned extensive are managed for a lower density, more pristine, and perhaps more leisurely experience opportunity, but may be beyond the reach of many tours that nonetheless may desire some experiences of that nature. Other extensive use zone experience opportunities include hikes up various volcanos and may appeal to those who wish to be physically challenged, develop outdoor skills, walk further, or have more solitude.

The establishment of good visitor management objectives and their corresponding zoning strategy requires periodic monitoring of visitor motivations, expectations, and preferences for experience opportunities and management techniques. It is expected that studies recently conducted in Galápagos (Wallace and Wurz, 1992) will reveal the need to refine and expand the current zoning system. The current zoning strategy may be too simple to meet the needs of the increased number of boats (the type, size, distance capability, and facilities of the boat one chooses affects the visitor's experience and may need to be linked with zoning strategy), visitors with varied preferences, local residents, and congestion at popular visitation sites, all of which are combined with complex resource and ecosystem constraints.

To illustrate zoning needs and possibilities, below there appears a hypothetical revised zoning spectrum for Galápagos and a detailed description of the management objectives, experience opportunities, and setting attributes for two of the zones.

ZONING SPECTRUM

Rural. Might include all areas adjacent to the park where the park is working with private landowners to develop activities such as lava tube tours on Santa Cruz, or equestrian and hiking trails that occur on a combination of park and private lands contiguously.

Intensive/recreational. Might include developed recreation areas in the park near local communities (Tortuga Bay) or park-related sites within communities. This could include guard stations and visitor centers, the Charles Darwin Foundation Research Station, port or transportation facilities, and other sites that include park personnel and activities and are designed for large numbers of visitors.

Intensive/natural. Would include visitation sites with outstanding wildlife, ecosystem, natural, or cultural history value, but with only moderate resource constraints. Higher use levels would be permitted (group size would still be site-specific, but tend toward larger groups) at sites of varying distances from port towns.

Extensive/natural. Would include sites with outstanding wildlife, ecosystem, natural or cultural history value, with more severe resource constraints (again, site-specific) limiting group size to smaller groups, or, conditions permitting, where a more leisurely experience with fewer encounters is desired. Sites of varying distances from port towns.

Semiprimitive. Back-country areas or remote beaches, usually on larger inhabited islands, more than one mile from any road or motorized beach landing area. Areas where foot, animal, or nonmotorized boat transport is required; risk, challenge, and required skills are greater. Resource constraints are low to moderate. Encounters with other visitors are kept low and both permits and Park Service orientation or special guides are required.

Pristine/scientific. Islands or parts of islands where ecosystem value is at its highest with no or very few exotic species introductions. Usually remote and uninhabited with severe resource constraints. Visits are very limited; usually but not always confined to scientists. Requires permits in advance and guides specially trained in low impact techniques. There would be many strict regulations.

Following is a more complete description for two of these categories, both of which would be new for Galápagos.

Intensive/recreational zone. *Management Objectives:* To provide easily accessible recreational, educational, and administrative areas near the park's gateway communities (ports) that accommodate large numbers of people, expose them to the larger goals and unique qualities of the park, and reduce the likelihood of inappropriate activities elsewhere in the park in locations that are primarily visited for nature tourism.

Experience Opportunities and Setting Attributes: Activities include swimming, sunbathing, boating, picnicking, some scenic viewing, affiliation with other visitors, visiting displays and educational exhibits, and making purchases related to the park.

Physical Setting: There are numerous roads, trails, boat docks, piers, and other structures present. Noise levels are moderate. The landscape affords views of natural areas in the distance, but is highly modified and "hardened" to accommodate many visitors. Water, electricity, and bathrooms are provided in the visitor centers and there are bathrooms at the beaches.

Social Setting: Both density and encounters with other visitors are high and local residents and tourists mix in a leisure setting. Park personnel are frequently seen and offer a variety of programs, talks, and assistance. A high level of security and amenities are offered in the park and there are a variety of lodging, food, and entertainment opportunities nearby.

Managerial Setting: There are almost no restrictions on party size, but other regulations, including hours of operation, are well posted. Admission fees are charged to some activities. Access to natural landscape areas is restricted by barriers, vegetation is planted and maintained, and park rangers use extensive education, law enforcement and cooperation with local authorities to achieve effective visitor management.

Semiprimitive zone. *Management Objectives:* To allow those visitors who seek a more self-directed or individualized experience (using outdoor skills in a natural setting) to have access to portions of the park where many natural features and values exist, but where concerns about species introduction are pressing and can be controlled more easily due to the proximity of ranger stations. To also reduce the pressure on intensive/natural zone visitation sites by dispersing opportunities for visitors wishing alternatives to traditional guided tours.

Experience Opportunities and Setting Attributes Activities: Hiking, camping, sea kayaking, volcano climbing, wildlife viewing, and nature study. There is the opportunity to use outdoor skills; moderate levels of risk and challenge and physical stamina are required.

Physical Setting: Remote, generally several miles away from traditional visitation sites or transportation corridors, in natural terrain that may have some mixture of endemic and exotic species, but very little other evidence of human activity. Rugged mountains, scrub forest, lava fields, or remote beaches may all be found within such a zone.

Social Setting: Groups will be no larger than five persons and all trails and campsites will have site quotas so that encounters should not exceed two other parties in a two-day period.

Managerial Setting: Permits are required and given on a first-come-first-serve basis. Itineraries are prepared and campsites assigned. Length of stay is from one to two days at any one site. Ranger patrols are regular, but their contact with visitors is optional and brief. Prior to entry visitors will watch a fifteen-minute videotape on low-impact techniques and backcountry regulations as well as undergo a check for exotic plant material and proper equipment.

As the examples begin to illustrate, once zones, or "opportunity classes," as they are sometimes called, are established, then site quotas (numbers of people or boats at one time), and other regulations appropriate for that setting, can be set. Carrying capacity (both biophysical and social capacity), then, is relative to the management objectives for a given zone, which in turn are based on some combination of ecological criteria and considerations about the balance or diversity of experience opportunities provided visitors in a given protected area. If Caleta Tortuga, a quiet cove not far from the airport at Baltra, provides an ideal spot for an uninterrupted and intimate experience with mangroves, then it might be zoned as an extensive/natural experience, even for day tours, which normally visit only busy places. Once so designated, it might have a daily site quota of perhaps only two to four parties a day, with a reservation system for morning and afternoon, to enable visitors to experience at least one site with only their group being present. Primitive or pristine experiences are frequently more remote, but some might be made more accessible through creative zoning. See Cifuentes (1992) for a similar zoning approach using different terminology. These types of zoning systems are slated for discussion during a workshop in Galápagos in February of 1993.

In Galápagos, it is important that concessionaires understand and help to manage whatever zoning system is developed. They can do this by participating in the planning process and then by making sure that visitor expectations, group size and behavior, equipment taken, and activities planned conform to those appropriate to a given zone or site. Though large boats will continue to use the park, once they enter a zone with site quotas or restrictions, they can send visitors ashore in smaller groups or to different sites within the area in order to conform with management objectives. In conjunction with zoning refinements, tour itineraries or reservation systems will have to address the regional distribution of tours in order to make it easier to comply with site quotas that may be developed.

It is a management principle in most protected areas that use in zones not managed for the integrity of specific setting attributes (especially group size, groups at one time, length of stay, equipment permitted, etc.), will gravitate toward busier, more developed settings with higher densities of people, increased evidence of human activity, and easier access. Tour operators must recognize that a well-planned zoning system provides quality to the visitor experience and more options that can enable the outfitter to adapt to market changes. Adventure tours, for example, rely greatly on lower density, more remote and pristine zones to provide a quality experience. In many areas where zoning is not present, adventure and ecotours are soon displaced by increased visitation and begin looking for the next "undiscovered" experience somewhere else. Even visitors who do not penetrate or spend much time in primitive zones appreciate knowing they exist (Dixon and Sherman, 1990).

Overriding management objectives for Galápagos will probably always favor a predominance of zones, such as the hypothetical intensive/natural and extensive/natural zones, which offer guided tours and well-marked trails that concentrate visitor impacts. This is likely to be complemented by moderate increases in developed recreational settings near communities and slow and careful increases in opportunities for some more primitive and pristine experiences. Pilot projects will have to carefully demonstrate the wisdom of this type of zoning for Galápagos. Because it is a world resource for studying evolution at the ecosystem level, more portions of the Galápagos than would be necessary in most parks will continue to be off limits to all but a highly selective group of scientists and other visitors.

It is only fair to note that the spectrum of opportunities is an inherent feature of most visitor management strategies and zoning in developed countries (Driver et al., 1988; Stankey et al., 1985 and 1979; Loomis and Graefe, 1992), but is just beginning to take hold in many developing protected areas and ecotourism sites and therefore will face any number of modifications. One excellent zoning concept that is being used in a few developing country protected areas is that of "village use zones" that identify areas traditionally important to local people for fishing, hunting, gathering, and limited resource extraction (fuel wood, for example, or sand) and are managed accordingly.

Limits of Acceptable Change

As implied above, setting a number which indicates the carrying capacity for a park or protected area is not very useful. Good zoning with site-specific regulations that fit both the site and the zone is much more informative. The concept of carrying capacity has evolved in several developed countries to become a more sophisticated measure of what is actually happening to a park's resources or the visitor experience. We know that there is no direct correlation between numbers of visitors and negative impacts that affect soil, vegetation, wildlife, or other people's experiences. The degree of impact depends on many variables in addition to the amount of use: the degree of site hardening (making landings, trails, or overlooks resistant to erosion, for example); the motivations and behavior of visitors; their mode of transport and lodging; the effectiveness of guides; group size; and environmental variables such as soil type, slope, vegetative types, and season of use. Perceptions of crowding and other social impact vary according to the zone being visited and what visitors expect to find there. It makes more sense to monitor impact and make changes in visitor management if unacceptable limits of negative impact are reached. One method for doing so is the Limits of Acceptable Change (LAC) process, which is briefly described below.

1. Select indicators for the management parameters that concern you the most at a given site in a given zone. These should be indicators directly related to the activities of visitors that can be controlled: soil erosion, site spreading, sea floor litter at mooring sites, stress on a particular wildlife species (the number of incidents of sea lion aggressiveness towards visitors in a given site in a six-month period might be an indicator, for example). Such indicators should be both biophysical and social in nature. Social indicators would be perceptions of crowding, the number of encounters with other groups per day at a site, the number of overbookings by tour operators, number of safety violations per month, number of people leaving donations at the visitor center, and so on. Indicators tell us how we are doing regarding some aspect of management.

 2. Establish standards for each indicator that set some limit of acceptable change. Some impacts are inevitable, but managers must be willing to say how much impact they will accept before changing the way they are managing. If trails are eroding faster than it is feasible to maintain them, if viewing areas are getting too wide, if some animals are changing their behavior in an unacceptable way, then management actions must be taken (party sizes reduced, viewing areas moved back, some sites hardened more than they are, or perhaps the overall number of visitors reduced). A standard for sea lion aggressiveness might be set at no more than three incidents per month for six consecutive months or some such definition depending on the best available information from those who understand sea lion behavior and the natural incidence of such aggressiveness.

 3. Monitor conditions and if acceptable limits are exceeded, make management changes that will bring resource or social conditions back within limits. Often current conditions are already unacceptable and must be corrected. If sea lion aggressiveness is unacceptable at intensively used visitor sites, it may be necessary to reroute a trail, to ask visitors to behave differently, or, in an extreme case, to change the opportunity class and zone (thereby reducing the number of visitors). Monitoring conditions requires that a park have good baseline data on existing conditions in order to be able to select indicators, set standards, and then to detect changes.

 The LAC approach forces managers to come to grips with the details of management in a way that goes far beyond any figure for overall carrying capacity. It is an important component in a sophisticated type of visitor management that can respond rationally to questions like those that have arisen in Galápagos about whether or not there are too many visitors, whether there is room in the "espacio turistico" (scheme of experience opportunities) for more tour operators, or whether or not developing a pilot site is too risky. Until protected area managers can develop (with concessionaires and others) and describe management objectives and then show specifically how sites within a park or reserve that correspond to those objectives are being impacted, it will be hard to make a case for changes in the type or number of concessionaires, group size, mode of transport, or many other management decisions. Capacity or limits are not static. They vary with changes in staff, budget, episodes of cholera, alterations in animal populations and increased stress levels brought on by the storms of El Niño, or with the changes in visitor expectations and preferences that occur over time. Concessionaires must be sensitive enough to realize that managers may have to change tour or site quotas if unacceptable limits are reached. The involvement of concessionaires in the planning process is also part of any LAC planning and will give them a sense of ownership in the visitor management strategies. For more on the LAC process, see Stankey et al. (1985).

TRAILS

Key elements in the management of visitors and concessions in Galápagos, or in any protected area, are the trail system and the guides, to which we will now turn. Trails are extremely important in any protected area and are almost never given the attention they need in new or developing protected areas or ecotourism sites. Most trails in the Galápagos are resistant to erosion and spreading, but those that are not are noticeably problematic. Trail maintenance and reconstruction can eat up a disproportionate amount of an area's budget. Proper trail route selection and design can avoid most of these problems, but is seldom done at the onset. Most trails form from use rather than by design. Concessionaires should be asked to participate in trail design and construction in order to impart a sense of the effort required to lay out a good trail and to increase the stewardship of trails. In the U.S. outfitters are often responsible for some portion of trail maintenance if they are primary users.

One of the most popular trails in Galápagos steeply climbs the hill at Bartolomé, the most famous photo site in the park. It was routed (or formed) in its current location on sandy soils, presumably in order to avoid nearby lava beds. The mobile and uncontained sandy soils, an often steep grade, and visitors who move to the side of the trail seeking firmer sand, have caused a huge eroded scar seen for miles. Had the trail originally been routed through the lava beds (which provide their own trail material), a proper grade utilized, and the sand contained near the summit, it would have been an almost unnoticeable, easy-to-maintain trail providing excellent interpretive opportunities en route. A trail rerouted in this way requires visitor education to keep people on a trail in the lava beds, but education costs less than restoration or trail construction in the long run. Good trails are also key to upgrading management capability in any area. Once built, control of group size and maintenance of drainage structures are far more important than the amount of trail use. Large groups do the most damage to trails in the Galápagos by causing site spreading as people bunch up on the trail to hear the guide or interpreter. Trail width and maintenance standards are also key "setting attributes" that change with different zones (primitive zones have more primitive trails in terms of width, difficulty, directions given, and levels of maintenance).

Selection and training of guides and interpreters. The dual categories of naturalist and auxiliary guides used in Galápagos has contributed to a de facto class structure and economic dichotomy that has led to friction among those who should be natural allies and concerned together about a marvelous place. Such a system is to be avoided and could be replaced instead by guides who share one category within which different grades of proficiency are recognized. In developing countries, for the present, advancement should be possible with or without formal educational degrees. This is not to say that standards and tests of knowledge and ability are not necessary or that degrees should not be encouraged. In fact, scholarships and other incentives are being developed in Galápagos to encourage local candidates to pursue formal education that includes second and third language training.

The park or protected area should remain centrally involved in guide training because a strong visitor and resource management component must be included if managers and concessionaires are to be partners. Furthermore, in Galápagos, park officials should be firmly in control of the licensing of guides who operate almost exclusively in this large park. With refinements in the management plan, resource management itself will become an increasingly important theme for interpretation. Guides and rangers can be mixed together for some portion of their training activities or internships and later during field interpretation activities; it is critical to further the idea of a shared mission and expertise. But incentives must be provided for good rangers to remain in the public sector since there is considerable economic pressure for the good ones to move to the private sector and become guides.

The guide system in Galápagos already has many positive aspects and has helped avoid many impacts, especially to wildlife and soils and vegetation near attraction sites. One thing that is immediately noticeable to the outsider familiar with interpretation, however, is that guides tend to focus on a rather narrow range of interpretation and talk largely about species of birds, reptiles, and plants. This is partially a result of visitor interest in species having shaped the guides' actions over time. It is also a result of school curricula that are still focused on taxonomy and the result, perhaps, of guide training that presents good information but goes light on practical demonstrations and exercises that incorporate less obvious themes into interpretive routines.

The fixation on species has contributed to the feeling held by concession-aires that the best sites are those with the most species and numbers of animals and that there is less to do at other sites. This has meant that animal-rich sites get visited frequently and tend to be the most congested, which is something that must be overcome as a new zoning scheme is developed. Galápagos has many other interpre-tive themes—vulcanism, geomorphology, ocean currents, climatology (El Niño), ecosystems, evolutionary theory, vulnerability of endemic organisms to invasion by exotics, gigantism, an incredible night sky, cultural history, importance to science—which if developed and used could turn most sites into interesting and exciting places. In other words, good guide training and selection and interpretive materials can actually have the effect of greatly expanding the number of what are considered desirable visitor sites and thereby lessen the pressure on overused sites—another lesson that might be applied to many areas (see Galápagos National Park, "Guides' Guide to the Visitor Sites," 1980).

EDUCATION AND OUTREACH WITH TOURISM INDUSTRY EMPLOYEES AND LOCAL COMMUNITIES

In many wildland protected areas, local people are asked to forgo the use of natural resources in order to protect resources for the public at large. In such areas the moral obligation to involve and provide compensation and benefits from conservation for local people, especially indigenous or traditional residents, is high (Wallace, 1992). In Galápagos, where only a small percentage of local people are natives and where incomes in general are higher than in the rest of Ecuador, this is less of an ethical issue, but an issue nonetheless. Any time the mechanisms for controlling growth are absent (the market trumps integrated planning unless done in advance) and people flock to an area that is booming, you only have a few days, it seems, before they, too, become "local" and decisions must be made in favor of their jobs and well-being—sometimes at the expense of resource protection. This makes outreach and education about the importance of the resource absolutely critical, and the sooner the better. Management capability includes the level of support from local people.

It is easy for politicians to take advantage of pressures that favor local well-being over the protection of the resource that brought the people in the first place. This is one of the most serious symptoms of the imbalance between private and public sector. This makes participation in local community affairs by park officials and park advocates absolutely essential, and the sooner the better.

Educational displays in the community; outreach into the schools; field trips; special occasions to invite locals into the park; special use areas for locals; inclusion of local representatives in park planning; the training and employing of locals in the park as staff, concessionaires, or tour guides; and asking park staff to stay active in local affairs, are all important tactics for managers to consider. Concessionaires can help greatly by doing conservation education with employees. Protected areas might even develop and require such training as one of the conditions for granting a permit. A fine example is already being set by the enlightened tour operators in Galápagos who give their employees—cooks, crewmen, mechanics—one day in every ten to accompany guided tours ashore to enjoy park resources and mix with guests while learning about the marvels of Galápagos. This is one small way to build local constituents who will be supporters of the resource and see it as more than making a living.

Park staff must be just as concerned about health, sanitation, education, and recreation in portal or port communities and work to assist communities to achieve their own management capability which is inseparable from that of the park's. Loaning labor and equipment to communities for such projects at key times is a good investment (Jardel, 1989).

Integrating Researchers and Nongovernmental Organizations into Protected Area Tourism Management

In Galápagos scientists have played a critical role in stabilizing and promoting protected area management and visitation. During the years 1981 to 1988, economic crisis in the Ecuadorian government virtually eliminated the budget for the National Park Service. Protection activities and visitation continued, however, because of the presence of the Charles Darwin Foundation Research Station and the contributions from international conservation groups and universities that were stimulated by the station (MacFarland, 1992). Scientific findings and activities are a part of what is interesting about Galápagos and are themselves visitor attractions. Scientists in Galápagos have been good about allowing small groups of tourists to see and even assist with their activities. Students come for a mixture of work and tourism.

Publications and media stimulated by research reach developed countries and stimulate the type of visitation that is compatible with the aims of area managers. And more recently, both Ecuadorian and foreign universities have provided labor and research needed by managers to solve management problems. Ecotourism is closely related to scientific tourism. It is up to protected area managers to make sure that research conducted in an area is relevant for the area and produces products and benefits that are spelled out before the research begins. International nongovernmental organizations have recently moved from an emphasis on designation of parks and protected areas to an emphasis on management. They are actively involved in managing some areas and the training of national agency personnel and nongovernmental organizations. They are an indispensable resource during times of budget shortfalls and during the formation of new ranger corps and administrative organizations.

CONCLUSION

Agencies responsible for protected area management in developing countries are still rarely given the power or resources to cope with the variety of threats to protected areas that slowly whittle away at area resources and which affect nearby communities. Given external debt, poverty, and scarce national resources, there is a compromising trend in developing countries, Ecuador being no exception, to simultaneously rely on natural resources to help pay foreign debts and also to cut costs by substituting nongovernmental organizations (conservation groups as well as ecotourism enterprises) as proxies for public land managers (Ashton, 1991; Boo, 1990).

Ecotourism concessions and nongovernmental organizations obviously provide an important complement to park management as this chapter has discussed. They should not, however, supersede or replace park administrators, rangers, or interpreters as those primarily responsible for the management of protected areas. There is no substitute for the long-term security and ecological and egalitarian management of protected areas that national and state systems—in this case the National Park Service in Galápagos—can provide (Wallace, Forthcoming; Barborak, 1992; Cornelius, 1991; Boo, 1990; MacKinnon, et al., 1990; McNeely and Thorsell, 1989). This is especially true in the case of protected areas that have national or international importance like Galápagos. Many of the problems that Galápagos National Park now faces are a result of private sector activities which moved ahead at a rate that far outdistanced the capability of the park to manage, and create their own momentum which became difficult to control.

However well meaning, tourism ventures operating in national protected areas are bought and sold; nongovernmental organizations and conservation groups change, lose their funding, fragment, or pass out of existence. Today's stewards are replaced by those who may be less interested in managing the "public trust." Wildlands like Galápagos that are precious resources for all time must be first protected with laws, public institutions, and management strategies that bridge the generations with all their social and political changes. Most ecotourism operations in the islands can only gain in the long run by slowing down and helping to strengthen the management capability of the Park Service in Galápagos which will be the long-term base upon which tourism rests. Park officials, on the other hand, must know that park management cannot be successful without the participation and sense of ownership and shared commitment by tour operators, nongovernmental organizations, and the other institutions that operate in and around the communities of Galápagos.

Hopefully this message has relevance for the relationship between tour operators and protected area managers in many places. The same imbalance exists in several places where this author has worked. Galápagos is already ahead of many areas. The Amazon, for example, could benefit from a Galápagos-like river and boat based ecotourism and park management strategy that could deliver visitors to the real Amazon protected areas and create an economic base for both parks and local people. Many current Amazon tours reach only jungle lodges in patches of secondary forest on private land and provide no benefits for long-term protection of the large intact ecosystems that will otherwise continue to be vulnerable to extractive economic forces. Those looking at the Galápagos case study presented here should recognize that this has been a relatively simple rendering of a complex and dynamic situation done by an outside observer. By the time this book is published, things will have changed there—old problems closer to being solved and new ones appearing.

I would like to close with a personal story. One day while working in Galápagos we were returning from Floreana and halfway to Santa Cruz. I was feeling very sick from dysentery. The Park Service boat captain summoned me from my bunk to see the fifteen or twenty dolphins that were running alongside and jumping incredibly high out of the water. We stopped and I managed to get on my mask and flippers and roll over the side—better to die with the dolphins. I went down thirty feet or so and they came swimming by powerfully, turning and cavorting but returning until they were swimming by close enough to touch. Light-headed, I went up for air and when I was ready to dive again we were miraculously joined by five sea lions that seemed much too far from land to be there. There we were, three species of large mammals, dancing and playing. I took off my glove and a playful sea lion pulled it way out of my reach as I tried to retrieve it. I lost track of time and the number of dives, but my condition put me into a dreamlike state where I was completely at home in such an unlikely place with such marvelous companions. It was a peak experience worth more than money can buy.

Protected areas like Galápagos are worth fighting for, and worth protecting for all people, for their own sake, for all time. It is an achievable goal and one that can be set in many places. May each of us return a little of what these places gives us to their care.

REFERENCES

Ashton, R. 1991. Presentation given at the Third Meeting of the National Tourism System, Manaus, Brazil (November).

Barborak, J. R. 1992. "Institutional Options for Managing Protected Area." Paper given at the IV World Congress on National Parks and Protected Areas. Caracas, Venezuela.

Boo, E. 1990. *Eco-tourism: The Potentials and Pitfalls.* Washington, D.C.: World Wildlife Fund.

Cifuentes, M. 1992. "Informe de Consulta Sometido a la Consideración del PNUD, Quito, Ecuador y de la Comisión Multisectoral Para Galápagos." Costa Rica: CATIE, Turrialba.

Cornelius, S. 1991. "Wildlife Conservation in Central America: Will it Survive the '90s?" Transcript from the 56th North American Wildland and Natural Resources Conference. Washington, D.C.: World Wildllife Fund U.S.

Cronin, L. 1990. "A Strategy for Tourism and Sustainable Development," in *World Leisure and Recreation*, vol. 32, no. 3, pp. 12–18.

Dixon, J. A., and P. B. Sherman. 1990. *Economics of Protected Areas: A New Look at Benefits and Costs.* Washington, D.C.: Island Press.

Driver, B. L., and P. J. Brown. 1975. "A Socio-psychological Definition of Recreation Demand With Implications for Recreation Resource Planning," in *Assessing Demand for Outdoor Recreation.* Washington, D.C.: National Academy of Sciences.

———. 1978. "The Opportunity Spectrum Concept in Outdoor Recreation Supply Inventories: A Rationale," in *Proceedings of Integrated Renewable Resource Inventory Workshop.* U.S. Forest Service General Technical Report RM-55, pp. 24–31.

Driver, B. L., P. J. Brown, G. H. Stankey, and T. G. Gregoire. 1987. "The ROS Planning System: Evolution, Basic Concepts, and Research Needed," in *Leisure Sciences*, vol. 9, no. 3, pp. 201–212.

Durst, P. 1988. "Nature Tourism: Opportunities for Promoting Conservation and Economic Development." Presented at the International Symposium on Nature Conservation and Tourism Development, Surat Than, Thailand (August).

Graefe, A. R., F. R. Kuss, and J. V. Vaske. 1990. "Directrices en el Impacto del Visitant: El Armanzon Formulado." Washington, D.C.: National Parks and Conservation Association.

Heberlein, T. A., and B. Shelby. 1977. "Carrying Capacity, Values and the Satisfaction Model: A Reply to Greist." *Journal of Leisure Research*, vol. 9, no. 2, pp. 142–148.

Izurieta, A. 1992. Personal communication with author, including diagrams and explanation of new patrol strategy during summer training session in Fort Collins, Colorado.

Jardel, E. P. 1989. "Estrategia para la Conservación de la Reserva de la Biosfera Sierra de Manatlan." El Grullo, Jalisco: Laboratoria Natural Las Joyas, Universidad de Guadalajara.

Loomis, L., and A. R. Graefe. 1992. "Overview of NPCA's Visitor Impact Management Process." Paper and workshop given at the IV World Congress on National Parks and Protected Areas, Caracas, Venezuela (February).

MacFarland, C. M. 1992. Personal communication with the author during the review of the manuscript.

MacFarland, C. M., G. Oviedo, P. Whelan, and V. Merino. 1991. "Ecuador: Biodiversity Conservation Through Strengthening of the Protected Areas System." Submitted to the Global Environmental Facility Project, Quito, Ecuador.

Machlis, G. E., D. A. Costa, and J. S. Cardenas. December 1990. "Galápagos Islands Visitor Study." Presented to the President's Commission, Quito, Ecuador.

MacKinnon, J., K. Child, and J. Thorsell, eds. 1990. *Managing Protected Areas in the Tropics*. Gland, Switzerland: International Union for the Conservation of Nature and Natural Resources (IUCN).

McNeely, J., and J. Thorsell. 1989. "Jungles, Mountains, and Islands: How Tourism Can Help Conserve the Natural Heritage." *World Leisure and Recreation*, Winter, vol. 31, no. 4, pp. 29–39.

Maldonado, L., 1992. Member of the President's Commission and administrator for Metropolitan Touring, interviewed at the World Ecotourism Conference, Belize City, Belize (November).

Manning, R. E. 1986. *Studies in Outdoor Recreation: A Review and Synthesis of the Social Science Literature*. Corvallis, Oreg.: Oregon State University Press.

Moore, A. 1987. "Diagnostico de la Situación del Turismo en Areas del Parque

Nacional Galápagos y su Proyección al Futuro." Quito, Ecuador.

———. 1992. Personal communication with the author who has been involved in the analysis of several carrying capacity studies in Galápagos.

President's High Level Commission (Comision de Alto Nivel). 1991. "Elementos Para Diseño del Plan Global de Turismo y Conservación Ecologica de Galápagos." Presidencia de la Republica, Quito, Ecuador.

Stankey, G. H., D. N. Cole, R. C. Lucas, M. E. Petersen, and S. S. Frissell. 1985. "The Limits of Acceptable Change (LAC) System for Wilderness Planning." USDA Forest Service General Technical Report, INT-176. Ogden, Utah: Intermountain Forest and Experiment Station.

Wallace, G. N. 1991. "Informe Sobre la Consultoria Al Grupo Tecnico y Comisión de Alto Nivel Para El Plan Global de Turismo y Conservación Ecologica de Las Islas Galápagos." Prepared for the United Nations Development Program, Quito, Ecuador (January).

———. 1992. "Real Ecotourism: Helping Protected Area Managers and Getting Benefits to Local People. Paper given at the IV World Congress on National Parks and Protected Areas, Caracas, Venezuela.

———. Forthcoming. "Wildlands in Latin America: A Need to Invest in the Development of National Protected Area Systems and Management." *Journal of Forestry.*

Wallace, G. N., and J. Wurz. 1992. "A Study of Visitor Motivations and Preferences of Experience Opportunities and Management in Galápagos National Park." Study in process at Colorado State University and the Charles Darwin Research Station, Fort Collins, Colorado.

Wallace, G. N., P. Tierney, and G. Haas. 1991. "The Right Link Between Wilderness and Tourism," in *Parks and Recreation*, September, vol. 25, no. 9, pp. 63–68.

Williams, P. 1991. "Eco-tourism Management Challenges." Paper given at the Travel Review Conference, Washington D.C. (February).

United Nations Development Programme. 1991. "Documento de Asistencia Preparatoria, INGALA/CONADE. Programa de las Naciones Unidas para el Desarrollo." Quito, Ecuador.

ACKNOWLEDGMENTS

Thanks to reviewers Kreg Lindberg, Alan Moore, George Stankey, and especially Craig MacFarland, president of the Charles Darwin Foundation, and Miguel Cifuentes, former superintendent of Galápagos, for their thoughtful reviews. I also wish to acknowledge the help of former and current park superintendents, Miguel Cifuentes, Fausto Cepeda, and Arturo Izurieta, for their ideas over the last three years and willingness to consider new approaches to management. We are grateful to the Darwin Foundation, Metropolitan Touring, and the U.S. Forest Service for their support of the ongoing research and work with the Park Service and commercial tour operators.

Economic Issues in Ecotourism Management

Kreg Lindberg and Richard M. Huber, Jr.

Ecotourism is a sizeable and growing industry for many countries. One of the primary advantages of ecotourism is that it provides an impetus to expand both conservation and tourism development. On the conservation side, ecotourism is the conservation benefit which is most easily sold and thus incorporated into decisions about land use. In concrete terms, entrance and other fees associated with ecotourism can supplement existing governmental conservation budgets and can provide incentives for private sector conservation. On the economic development side, ecotourism can bring employment opportunities to remote regions. In addition, it is generally assumed that ecotourism requires less public sector infrastructure investment than does more traditional tourism (though there may be correspondingly fewer benefits; a rigorous evaluation of investment required for each job created or dollar of foreign exchange earned in the respective sectors remains to be undertaken).

However, many observers voice the concern that ecotourism has not reached its potential as a tool of conservation or economic development, in part because many worthwhile projects cannot find financing, in part because host countries have yet to receive the full revenue potential inherent in ecotourism, and in part because relatively little of the revenue which has been generated has directly supported conservation and economic development.

In an effort to expand ecotourism's contribution, this chapter outlines strategies for:

- setting tourism fees;

- using these fees to finance ecotourism development and traditional conservation management; and

- increasing ecotourism's contribution to the economic development of communities near ecotourism destinations.

There is tremendous variation between locations not only with respect to the ecotourism attractions themselves but also with respect to socioeconomic and political conditions. Therefore, this chapter outlines basic principles, together with a mix of strategies for achieving common economic goals relating to ecotourism. Each location must determine its economic objectives and choose the management strategies which best meet those objectives.

Collecting and utilizing basic information must be part of that process. Ecotourism will provide the greatest benefits, and thus best meet objectives, when management is informed. Unfortunately, there has been little rigorous data collection and analysis. Information needs are discussed in this chapter, and effective management will require collection and utilization of this data. In fact, this information will often be crucial simply to initially justify ecotourism as an alternative to activities such as traditional tourism or unsustainable resource extraction.

TOURISM FEES: REVENUE OBJECTIVES AND DEMAND ESTIMATION

Managers of many natural areas have turned to tourism fees as a mechanism for recovering visitor management costs, as well as the costs of traditional conservation management or community development programs. However, the revenue generation opportunities provided by ecotourism have yet to be fully achieved (Wells, 1992; Lindberg, 1991).

The primary focus of this chapter will be on setting fees for foreign visitors since such decisions can be made on the relatively straightforward basis of maximizing the economic benefit to the host country. Lower fees for domestic residents can be justified on the grounds of both economic efficiency and equity (Lindberg, 1991), but such decisions often also include social and political considerations beyond the scope of this chapter. Readers interested in the experience of the United States and Canada regarding pricing for domestic visitation should refer to Aukerman (1990), Walsh (1986) and Rosenthal et al. (1984). Child and Heath (1990) also question the appropriateness of developing countries subsidizing foreign visitors through low fees.

Several countries, including Peru, Ecuador, and Kenya, have raised fees for foreigners while maintaining lower fees for residents (Olindo, 1991). Such differential pricing is common within the traditional tourism industry. For example, airlines often charge more for tickets purchased close to the departure date, based on the premise that such travelers have greater willingness to pay and less flexibility. Likewise, hotels often reduce rates during the off-season in response to variations in seasonal demand.

In effect, parks and similar facilities will need to act like businesses when providing tourism opportunities to foreigners. Such behavior often requires bureaucratic, and occasionally legal, changes. At the same time, parks need to continue traditional activities, such as conservation and, where appropriate, provision of subsidized recreation to residents.

Fee levels will depend in large part on national and local objectives. Two possible objectives are to charge fees which equal the cost of providing the service (cost recovery) or to charge fees that will generate as much profit as possible (thereby providing revenue to finance traditional conservation activities). There may be additional objectives, which may modify or replace these two. For example, fees may be kept low to encourage increased visitation and thereby increased economic opportunities for tourism-related businesses in the region. Alternatively, fees may be raised to encourage the private sector to develop ecotourism facilities that would not be profitable as long as fees for "public" destinations were kept artificially low.

Regardless of which objective is chosen, knowledge of demand for the ecotourism attraction will be necessary to set fees. That is, how many tourists will visit the attraction and how much are they willing to pay? Methods for estimating this demand will be described after the following discussion of management objectives. Case study examples of pricing for different objectives follow the methods section.

MANAGEMENT OBJECTIVE 1: COST RECOVERY

The focus of this objective is to set tourism fees such that they generate enough revenue to pay for providing the ecotourism opportunity. Fees should, at the minimum, offset capital costs (such as construction of a visitor center) and operating costs (such as maintenance of facilities, salaries for guides, and so on). Ideally, they should also offset such "indirect" costs as the cost of ecologic damage and the cost of negative impact on local communities, though such costs are difficult to quantify.

MANAGEMENT OBJECTIVE 2: PROFIT MAXIMIZATION

The focus of this objective is to set fees such that they generate as much profit as possible. Fees should more than offset the cost of providing the tourism opportunity. The profits (revenues minus costs) can then be used to help finance traditional conservation activities, subsidized recreation opportunities to residents, or other program objectives. In practice, there is often insufficient information to accurately determine the financial, not to mention the ecologic or social, costs of ecotourism. Since both of the above objectives require knowledge of these costs when setting fees, a high priority should be placed on obtaining accurate cost information (see page 103, Some General Principles for Tourism Fee Policy).

Managers trying to maximize *profits* should keep in mind that this goal is not the same as maximizing *revenues*. Revenue maximization generally results in trying to attract as many tourists as possible, but profit maximization may occur at lower visitation levels since the financial, ecologic, and social costs of ecotourism can increase more quickly than revenues at high visitation levels.

OTHER MANAGEMENT OBJECTIVES

From the purely financial viewpoint of the attraction owner, ecotourism opportunities for foreigners should only be provided if fees at least cover costs. However, additional objectives may lead owners, particularly governmental owners, to provide opportunities even when costs are not covered. For example, fees may be kept low to maintain high levels of visitation, thereby providing economic opportunities to tourism businesses (however, the resulting loss of fee revenue should be explicitly recognized and justified). Or fees for foreigners may not be sufficient to cover all costs, but they may generate sufficient revenue to help subsidize domestic visitation.

Benefits such as generation of employment or domestic recreation opportunities can be substantial. For example, Tobias and Mendelsohn (1991) estimated that the privately-run Monteverde Reserve was worth between $97,500 and $116,200 per year as a recreation site for Costa Rican residents.

Conversely, high fees can be used not only to raise revenue but also to limit or disperse visitors when particular sites have become crowded (Bamford et al., 1988). Kenya, for example, has considered charging higher fees at crowded attractions in an effort to disperse visitors to less visited attractions; of course, this strategy requires that similar attractions be available for visit (Leakey, 1990; EIU, 1991). A similar strategy has been recommended for Nepal (Gurung, 1990 as cited in Wells, 1992). In addition, experience in the United States suggests that high fees will reduce litter and vandalism at natural areas (Aukerman, 1990).

These strategies implicitly depend on a tradeoff between price and visitation levels: as the price is increased, the number of visitors will decrease, and vice versa. This is a basic economic principle that should not be ignored, but current fees are so low for most attractions that even substantial increases will likely have little impact on demand *in terms of choosing a destination*. Tourist surveys, as well as actual tourist behavior, suggest that price is a relatively unimportant factor when choosing an ecotour, and that even when price is a concern tourists are willing to pay high fees if they know that these fees are being used to enhance their experience or to conserve the special area they have come to see (Lindberg, 1991; Aukerman, 1990; Bovaird, 1984). Several parks have raised their fees without noticeably affecting visitor levels and many more are able to do so. In fact, if these revenues are then used to improve the attraction, demand will probably increase.

Price may play a more important role *in terms of choosing activities* at the destination. That is, an increase in fees at all parks in Kenya may have a relatively small impact on the number of ecotourists going to Kenya, but an equivalent increase only at crowded sites may encourage tourists to go to less crowded sites within Kenya.

Achieving any of these management objectives requires that there be sufficient tourists willing to pay fees high enough to meet objectives. Managers should remember that demand for ecotourism can be very unpredictable and dependent on factors beyond their control. However, the following methods can be used for estimating this demand.

Method 1: market evaluation. The basic concept behind this method is that a given attraction can expect levels of visitation and a willingness to pay fees equivalent to existing attractions which are similar in consumer appeal, cost of travel, and other "demand factors" (see Figure 4-1 for a list of common demand factors for ecotourists). This method is a common basis for determining whether investments in the private sector will be worthwhile (see Smith, 1989, for a discussion of its application in the tourism field). However, care must be taken to evaluate how new facilities expand the supply of destinations, thereby putting downward pressure on prices for both existing and new facilities. Unfortunately, lodges and other ecotourism businesses typically do not share information on visitation levels and prices, so comparison is difficult. In addition, few national parks and other "public" facilities have historically charged such fees; when fees have been charged, they have rarely been based on business considerations such as the cost of providing the service and the willingness of consumers to pay for the service. Even private reserves, which generally charge more than public parks, often set low fees since costs are partially underwritten by other programs, such as scientific research and foundation grants (Alderman, 1990).

Even when data is obtained from similar facilities, they must be adjusted to take into account differences in demand factors, such as quality of attraction and travel cost. Ideally, it will be possible to identify an attraction which ranks roughly the same on all factors. More likely, however, is that rankings will be different and judgment must be used to estimate the optimal fee. One recent example is an estimate that the appropriate user fee for typical parks in Central America is between $5.00 and $10.00 per day (Ashton and Haysmith, 1992). This estimate is based on ranking Central American parks relative to parks in Africa and elsewhere. Central American parks would rank lower in terms of quality of attraction (ease of viewing wildlife, etc.) and better in terms of cost of travel to the destination country (at least for the U.S. market). Considering all factors, $5.00 to $10.00 was viewed as an appropriate fee range.

Currently, because there has been little systematic analysis of demand factors for ecotourism, the importance of each demand factor must be largely based on intuitive judgment by those familiar with the industry. In the future, however, additional research may help identify the importance of each factor, thus facilitating wider application of this strategy. Parks could then base their fees on those charged at other sites which are most similar in terms of important demand factors; differences in less important factors would have less effect on setting fees. Initial results from a

Figure 4–1. Common Demand Factors

INTERNATIONAL FACTORS

Income. Richer tourists generally travel more and pay higher prices.

Population. More total tourists generally means greater demand for specific sites.

Tastes. Demand for ecotourism vacations is dependent on the level of awareness and concern about environmental conservation.

**Destination Image.* Attractions with strong positive images in source countries will lure more tourists. Costa Rica and Belize have excellent reputations within the United States tourism market. Popular animals such as gorillas and large carnivores will generate high demand.

Competing Attractions. The more unique an attraction is, the higher fees it will be able to charge. Rwanda's gorillas, Nepal's Mount Everest, and Ecuador's Galápagos are unique and high-priced attractions.

Cost of Travel (time and money) to the Destination Country. The lower the cost of travel from the source country to the destination country, the higher the demand.

NATIONAL/LOCAL FACTORS

**Quality of Attraction.* Sites that include attractions which are appealing, diverse, and easy to view will be relatively popular (this factor is essentially the extent to which "destination image" is actually experienced).

**Quality of General Trip Experience.* Trips which provide higher quality experiences will be able to charge higher fees. Quality is based on factors such as whether lodging is clean and comfortable, food is safe and enjoyable, guides and other employees are friendly and informed, sites are uncrowded, and so on.

Political and Economic Stability. Tourists prefer traveling in stable countries. Tourism in Guatemala, Sri Lanka, Peru, Rwanda, and Nepal has decreased during periods of instability.

**Complementary Attractions.* There will be more demand for sites with popular attractions nearby. Demand for parks in Ecuador and Peru is supplemented by the availability of traveling to Machu Picchu in the same vacation.

**Cost of Travel (time and money) from the Gateway to the Attraction.* Attractions that are more convenient to major cities and existing tourism circuits will receive greater demand.

*These factors can often be affected through careful planning and management.

Source: Expanded from Lindberg, 1991; Ashton and Haysmith, 1992.

Costa Rican survey (Baldares and Laarman, 1990) suggest that the following factors affect the appropriate fee level: tourist income, quality of the experience, tourist's age and years of education, and the number of other protected areas visited in Costa Rica (the latter two factors may represent taste).

Likewise, surveys of tourists at Maasai Mara National Reserve and Amboseli National Park in Kenya (Henry, Waithaka, and Gakahu, 1992; Henry and Western, 1988) suggest that quality of attraction is the most important factor, followed by quality of general trip experience and political and economic stability.

Despite the lack of information, market evaluation can often be implemented. In Costa Rica, for example, fees charged at the private Monteverde Cloud Forest Reserve could serve as an example for fees at national parks. Monteverde is not run strictly as a business, and the facilities there are more extensive than in national parks, but the fact that Monteverde charges fees many times as great as the national parks suggests that the parks could also raise fees.

Method 2: survey of tourist demand. The basic concept behind this method is that tourists estimate their own demand for the attraction in response to specific survey questions. A survey of this type in Costa Rica revealed that both Costa Ricans and foreigners agreed that entrance fees to the three most popular national parks (and to Monteverde) should be raised (Baldares and Laarman, 1990). Furthermore, both Costa Ricans and foreigners agreed that foreigners should pay more than residents, even though that was not government policy.

Surveyors asked tourists, "For the type of visit you are making here ... how much should be the normal entrance fee for visitors who come from outside of Costa Rica?" Figure 4-2 is a compilation of the results. An examination of the graph shows that the majority of both residents and nonresidents felt that nonresidents should pay more than the 25 colones ($0.30) actually charged. Several respondents felt that the fee should be greater than $2.40. This information can be statistically analyzed to more accurately determine the revenue maximizing fee (see Method 3), but a visual evaluation of Figure 4-2 suggests that a fee of approximately $1.20 should be charged to nonresidents.

The weakness of this method is that the results likely underestimate actual demand and thus the potential fee level. In part this is due to the general difficulties in obtaining accurate responses to surveys (tourists often underestimate what they would actually be willing to pay). In addition, the surveyors note that responses might have been higher if the survey had been administered during the summer months rather than winter months. Furthermore, the responses might have differed if questions had been phrased differently. For example, a minority of the actual respondents indicated that they felt the appropriate fee should be $2.40 or higher. However, if the question had been rephrased to, "If the entrance fee was $2.40, would you have canceled your trip to the park?," it is likely that the majority of respondents would have indicated a willingness to pay this higher fee.

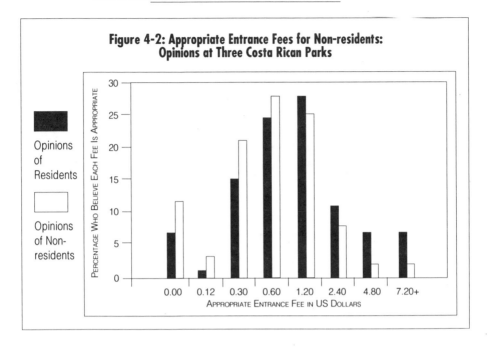

Figure 4-2: Appropriate Entrance Fees for Non-residents: Opinions at Three Costa Rican Parks

Method 3: demand curve analysis. Probably the most accurate strategy is to set fees using demand curve analysis. A demand curve measures how much tourists are willing to pay to see the attraction, as well as the trade off between price and number of visitors. Demand curves thereby enable managers to identify the revenue-maximizing fees.

Demand curves have been estimated for developing country parks using the hedonic pricing method (Edwards, 1987) and the travel cost method (Tobias and Mendelsohn, 1991; Durojaiye and Ikpi, 1988). However, surveys of the type discussed under Method 2, but designed and administered to contingent valuation standards, will generally be simpler and easier to apply in a wide range of settings. Researchers can extend the analysis presented in Method 2 by using statistical analysis to estimate the revenue-maximizing fee. In the Costa Rican case, the maximizing fee was estimated at $1.20. As noted above, this estimate is considered low.

Method 4: market-based reactive management and auctions. The basic concept of this method is to react to the tourism market as flexibly as possible by changing fees as demand changes. Because of the inherent imprecision in estimating demand, as well as the fickleness of the industry, this method is an important supplement to the three already discussed. That is, fees might be set at $10 based on tourist surveys or evaluation of equivalent attractions. However, if the number of visitors continues to increase rapidly, managers should consider raising fees. Likewise, if the number of visitors decreases rapidly, managers should consider lowering fees. In addition, if managers cannot use one of the first three methods to estimate demand, they can use reactive management to gradually increase fees until their goals are met (cost recovery, profit maximization, and so on).

Auctioning permits or other tourism fees will typically align fees with demand since tour operators will bid as much as they are willing to pay for the permit (provided that the auction is effectively administered). However, auctions are generally appropriate only when there is a limited number of permits or allowable entries and when the price of such permits is relatively high. This will usually be the case with hunting and such high-value tourism opportunities as viewing mountain gorillas in Rwanda.

The difficulty with reactive management within the context of government-run ecotourism attractions is that agencies rarely have the necessary flexibility to quickly react to changes in the marketplace. However, the benefits of such flexibility can be a powerful force for decentralization of authority to set fees.

The most appropriate method for setting fees will depend on local conditions, availability of resources to undertake surveys and analysis, and other considerations. In particular, estimating demand for new facilities will generally involve Methods 1 or 4 since they do not require a stream of current tourists.

TOURISM FEES: FINANCING ECOTOURISM AND CONSERVATION PROGRAMS

Estimated revenues need to be compared with costs to determine whether management objectives will be met (e.g., cost recovery or profit maximization). This comparison will often take the form of a financial analysis or benefit-cost analysis, especially if a loan is sought to cover costs. Such analysis is presented in the first case study.

CASE 1: COST RECOVERY AT THE ST. LUCIA SULPHUR SPRINGS

The St. Lucia Sulphur Springs are located on the Caribbean island/nation of St. Lucia. Tourism to St. Lucia has increased roughly 10 percent a year for the past eight years, with 24 percent of all arrivals spending time to visit the Sulphur Springs National Landmark, an area of boiling hot springs, volcanic promontories, and tropical vegetation. In an effort to improve the island's tourism product, the St. Lucia Tourism Board, in conjunction with the Organization of American States (OAS), analyzed whether tourism fee revenues would be sufficient to recover costs of enhancing the attraction (Huber and Park, 1991).

The analysis includes cost estimates for the infrastructural, educational, and environmental projects necessary for the rehabilitation of the natural landmark (see Table 4-1). Capital costs include the construction of a visitor center, restaurant, rest

Table 4-1. Sample IRR Analysis for the St. Lucia Sulphur Springs
(all values in EC$; US$1=EC$2.7)

YEAR	1991	1992	1993	1994	1995	1996	1997	1998	1999	2000	2001	2002	2003
COSTS OF PROJECT													
Capital, Maintenance, Programming	46,000	717,760	142,000	65,000	65,000	65,000	65,000	65,000	65,000	65,000	65,000	65,000	65,000
Additional Personnel		55,200	55,200	55,200	55,200	55,200	55,200	55,200	55,200	55,200	55,200	55,200	55,200
Total Costs	46,000	772,960	197,200	120,200	120,200	120,200	120,200	120,200	120,200	120,200	120,200	120,200	120,200
ADDITIONAL REVENUE RESULTING FROM PROJECT													
Increased Visits	0	18,514	39,806	64,198	49,915	27,411	3,781	**					
Increased Price	0	155,520	163,296	171,461	180,034	189,036	198,487	200,000	200,000	200,000	200,000	200,000	200,000
Revenue from Concessions	0	48,878	53,766	59,142	60,000	60,000	60,000	60,000	60,000	60,000	60,000	60,000	60,000
Total Additional Revenue	0	222,912	256,868	294,801	289,949	276,447	262,268	260,000	260,000	260,000	260,000	260,000	260,000
NET REVENUE FROM PROJECT (additional revenue minus costs)	-46,000	-550,048	59,668	174,601	169,749	156,247	142,068	139,800	139,800	139,800	139,800	139,800	139,800

**The annual number of visitors was limited to 100,000, so increased visits disappear in 1998, the year in which visitation is expected to reach 100,000 even without the project.

Internal rate of return (IRR) for the project: 19.3%

room facilities, and an environmental education room with exhibits. Additional costs include maintenance and programming. Furthermore, a tourism assistant and four maintenance staff will be hired (existing staff includes a manager and tour guides).

The costs of this enhancement are expected to be recovered through three avenues. First, the enhanced quality of the attraction is expected to cause an increase in visits. Second, entrance fees will be raised from EC$3 (approximately $1) to EC$5. St. Lucian groups will be admitted free with prior arrangement. Third, revenues will be earned from restaurant, handicraft, and other concessions.

The authors of this feasibility study employed modified versions of Methods 1 and 2 to estimate appropriate tourism fees and thereby determine whether revenues would cover the cost of the investment. They surveyed visitors to the region to determine whether tourists were interested in the improvements under consideration. These surveys (similar to the sample survey in Figure 4-3) and historical visitation data demonstrated that: the sulphur springs was already one of the most popular attractions on the island; most tourists would stay longer if facilities were available; and last, several specific facilities, such as a visitor center, interpretive panels, and restaurant, were desired. Based on survey results, and knowledge of similar attractions, the authors estimated that there would be an increase in tourists and that tourists would be willing to pay the higher entrance fee for an enhanced attraction.

Once the costs and revenues associated with the project were estimated, the authors used financial analysis to predict whether the project would be worthwhile. Financial analysis techniques will only be briefly covered here; interested readers should refer to Brealey and Myers (1988) or similar references for more information. Financial analysis is based on the straightforward concept that projects should only be undertaken if they are profitable, that is, if the benefits of those projects outweigh the costs (net benefits are positive). When more than one alternative produces positive net benefits, the alternative with the highest net benefit should be chosen.

Project benefits and costs usually occur over a number of years. One of the central concepts in economic analysis is that future benefits and costs are worth less than the same benefits and costs that occur today. Discounting is the process whereby these future benefits and costs are reduced to a present-day value. Projects can then be evaluated on the basis of their "internal rate of return" (IRR), "net present value" (NPV), or similar criterion. The IRR is determined by calculating the "rate of return" (a discount rate) that just equalizes benefits and costs over the life of the project (that is, the present value of all benefits minus costs is zero). When the IRR is higher than the cost of borrowing money, the project is profitable and worthwhile to undertake.

The NPV is the net value of a project (benefits minus costs) in current dollars (or other currency) over the life of the project, given a specific interest rate or discount rate. A positive NPV is equivalent to an IRR greater than the cost of borrowing money. Although NPV is a more robust decision-making tool than IRR, IRR is more intuitive.

Figure 4-3. Sample Questions to Determine Viability of Expanding Infrastructure and Services

Management Goal #1: To collect baseline information about visitors.

Question: In which country do you live?

Question: How many times have you visited this country?

Management Goal #2: To determine the level of interest in ecotourism destinations.

Question: Have you visited any national parks or other natural attractions in this country?

If yes, which ones?

If no, would you be interested in doing so on future visits?

Very Probably ❏ Probably ❏ Possibly ❏ Probably not ❏ Don't Know ❏

Management Goal #3: To determine the level of interest in supplemental attractions.

Question: Would you be interested in visiting a botanic garden, archaeological site, historical museum, or other natural or cultural attraction?

Very Probably ❏ Probably ❏ Possibly ❏ Probably not ❏ Don't Know ❏

Management Goal #4: To determine whether investment in additional facilities should be considered.

Question: Would you spend one to three days of a future visit in the area of this park if more amenities or facilities were available?

Very Probably ❏ Probably ❏ Possibly ❏ Probably not ❏ Don't Know ❏

Question: What facilities or services do you feel would greatly improve the quality of your experience here?

1. Picnic Area	4. Information signs	7. Brochures
2. Restaurant/Bar	5. Hiking trails	8. Other (please list)
3. Visitor Center	6. Trail guides	_____

Question: If we were to develop these facilities or services, would you be willing to pay higher fees for the higher quality experience?

Source: Adapted from Huber and Park, 1991.

Both criteria are based on the same information, however, and can be calculated using computer spreadsheet programs such as Lotus 123, Excel, or Quattro Pro.

Returning to the Sulphur Springs example (Table 4-1), the estimated costs are expected to outweigh the estimated benefits in the first two years of operation (negative "Net Revenue From Project"). Thereafter, the project will generate more revenues than costs. The expected IRR of this project is 19.3 percent, which is sufficiently high to justify financing.

It should be noted that this case study involves *expected* costs and revenues, rather than actual performance. Destinations such as gorilla tourism in Rwanda have demonstrated ecotourism's ability to earn profits. The St. Lucia example here was used because it is a more "typical" destination, and thus illustrates the expected ability to recover costs with even modest fees.

Recovery of costs in providing the ecotourism experience will generally be the minimum criterion. However, at some destinations revenue will exceed costs, with the resulting profits available for conservation programs, funding of other government programs, and so on. The high fees for gorilla tourism in Rwanda and Galápagos tourism in Ecuador, for example, are used in part to fund traditional conservation activities within the park systems. Table 4-2 and Figure 4-4 show that gorilla tourism has not only paid for park management but has also generated substantial profits for the government's treasury. In Kenya, tourism revenues are expected to soon cover the total cost of managing the country's parks and reserves. Likewise, tourism at Kota Kinabalu Park in Sabah, Malaysia, generates sufficient funds to cover the entire Sabah Parks budget.

CASE 2: PROFIT MAXIMIZATION AT PARKS IN ZAMBIA AND RWANDA

Two case studies from Africa employ Method 4 in targeting revenue maximizing tourism fees. Since the visitor level is controlled and relatively low in each case, these projects have likely also targeted profit maximization.

As part of Zambia's Lupande Development Project, local safari hunting concessions for South Luangwa National Park are auctioned to tour operators (Lewis, Kaweche, and Mwenya, 1990). Assuming the auction is held competitively, this method of selling hunting rights maximizes fee revenues. Proceeds from hunting concessions (and profits from hippopotamus sales) are then channeled through a "wildlife conservation revolving fund," with 60 percent being used for managing wildlife and 40 percent being given to local chiefs for community projects.

Hunting concession fee revenues earmarked for wildlife management in 1987 were K146,000 ($18,250), which was sufficient to cover the recurrent costs of $17,625 incurred by the village scout program, construction and maintenance, supplies, and public relations. Other governmental agencies also benefitted through safari hunting licenses (which are charged in addition to the concessions and which

Table 4-2. Maximizing Revenue from Tourism Fees: The Case of Rwanda's Gorilla Tourism
(All figures in US Dollars)

YEAR	1976	1977	1978	1979	1980	1981	1982	1983	1984	1985	1986	1987	1988	1989
FEE INCOME	7,072	8,954	10,195	12,240	36,513	88,837	114,917	135,281	261,198	298,780	348,276	378,821	512,195	1,000,000
EXPENSES	16,027	20,716	34,244	44,625	56,633	84,210	95,410	97,405	113,873	187,847	168,791	196,586	197,561	197,561
PROFIT/(LOSS)	(8,955)	(11,762)	(24,049)	(32,385)	(20,120)	4,627	19,507	37,876	147,325	110,933	179,485	182,235	314,634	802,439

Note: Expenses include salaries for guides and guards.

Source: Ministere de Plan, 1989; Vedder and Weber, 1990.

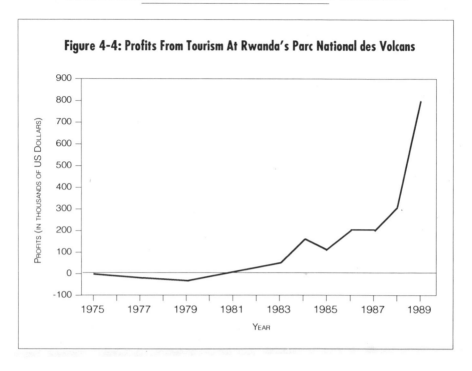

Figure 4-4: Profits From Tourism At Rwanda's Parc National des Volcans

totaled $36,130 in 1987), sales of elephant ivory, and fines collected from arrested poachers.

Rwanda's Parc National des Volcans has generally pursued market-based reactive management in setting fees for visitation of the mountain gorillas. The popularity of visiting the gorillas resulted in demand far exceeding the visitation limit set at approximately twenty-four tourists per day. This excess demand led the government to increase fees to almost $200 per person for a one-hour visit, thereby generating revenues of roughly $1 million in 1989 (Vedder and Weber, 1990). Because excess demand still existed until civil war closed down gorilla tourism, the government could probably have increased fees further (although they may have to revise fees downward as gorilla tourism is developed in Uganda and Zaire; such a revision has already occurred in the process of switching from pricing in Rwandan francs to pricing in U.S. dollars).

Even with the visitation limit, gorilla tourism generated substantial profits. Official figures and informed estimates demonstrate that tourism has not only paid for the cost of guides but has also financed park guards and generated profits for the central government treasury (see Table 4-2 and Figure 4-4). For example, in 1989 tourism fees generated $1,000,000 in revenue while park expenses were less than $200,000. In this manner, ecotourism fees have financed not only ecotourism but also conservation and general government programs.

CASE 3: INCORPORATING OTHER MANAGEMENT OBJECTIVES IN PRICING TREKKING TOURISM IN NEPAL

Decisions to maintain low fee levels in order to attain other management objectives will reduce fee revenues. However, innovative strategies such as multitiered pricing structures can be implemented to minimize lost revenue. For example, the country of Nepal currently charges fees of $10,000 for climbing Mount Everest and $8,000 for climbing other 8,000-meter peaks. Beginning in the autumn of 1993, the fee for Everest will increase to a range between $50,000 and $70,000 depending on group size (Anonymous, 1992; Noland, 1992). At the same time, fees for the more casual treks undertaken by the majority of tourists will be doubled, but still remain relatively low at $15 to $25 per week. This combination of fees will likely sustain demand for the small-scale tourism businesses dependent on large numbers of trekkers while maintaining governmental fee revenues at fairly high levels.

TOURISM FEES: A DECISION MAKING PROCESS

The previous sections outlined common objectives and methods, together with examples of how specific destinations have used tourism fees to raise revenue. This section outlines a generic decision making process for determining tourism fees. As illustrated in Figure 4-5, the first step is to determine fee objectives (cost recovery, profit maximization, or alternative criterion). The second step is to estimate whether revenues will be sufficient to cover costs. If so, prices should be set appropriately. If not, decision makers must determine whether goals such as provision of local employment or recreation opportunities will be sufficiently great to justify providing ecotourism opportunities at a financial loss. If so, additional funding must be found to cover these losses. Regardless of objective chosen, results should be monitored to determine whether objectives are being met.

INCORPORATING BROADER ECONOMIC AND SOCIAL IMPACTS

This chapter has primarily focused on analysis of projects as if they were run like businesses. That is, the decision maker is only concerned with the financial costs and benefits accruing to the project. In some cases, it will be appropriate to analyze government projects on the same basis, but governments are often interested in broader social costs and benefits such that the analysis needs to be expanded.

One method for doing so, the economic internal rate of return (EIRR), is based on the concept that market prices do not always reflect the true economic cost or benefit to society, in part because of public subsidies and taxes or control of prices and wage rates. As a result, EIRR uses "economic" prices rather than market prices. In practical terms, this means that: international (border) prices will be used for traded

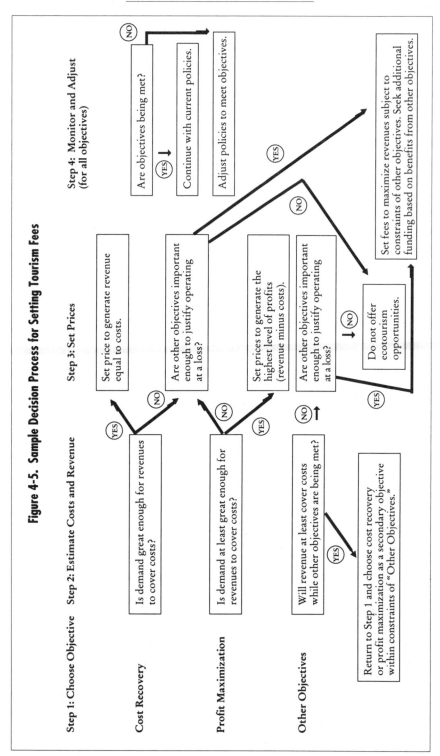

Figure 4-5. Sample Decision Process for Setting Tourism Fees

Step 1: Choose Objective   Step 2: Estimate Costs and Revenue   Step 3: Set Prices   Step 4: Monitor and Adjust (for all objectives)

Cost Recovery

Is demand great enough for revenues to cover costs?

Set price to generate revenue equal to costs.

Are other objectives important enough to justify operating at a loss?

Profit Maximization

Is demand at least great enough for revenues to cover costs?

Set prices to generate the highest level of profits (revenue minus costs).

Are other objectives important enough to justify operating at a loss?

Do not offer ecotourism opportunities.

Other Objectives

Will revenue at least cover costs while other objectives are being met?

Return to Step 1 and choose cost recovery or profit maximization as a secondary objective within constraints of "Other Objectives."

Set fees to maximize revenues subject to constraints of other objectives. Seek additional funding based on benefits from other objectives.

Are objectives being met?

Continue with current policies.

Adjust policies to meet objectives.

goods (such as imported food for tourists), with appropriate adjustments for transport and handling costs; shadow prices will be used for nontraded goods (such as labor); and transfer payments (such as duties or taxes) are excluded.

The second method, social benefit-cost analysis (SBCA), extends EIRR by recognizing that many benefits (and costs) are important to society, but do not have "economic" value in the sense that they are bought and sold in markets. In fact, public funding of parks and protected areas has relied primarily on the fact that natural areas provide such benefits as watershed protection, species conservation, recreation, and others (Dixon and Sherman, 1990; McNeely, 1988).

These benefits are, of course, much more difficult to value than fee revenues, but much progress has been made in doing so. Once the benefits and costs are estimated into the future, the project is analyzed using the NPV or IRR criterion. However, the discount rate for social projects is usually lower than the rate used for financial projects. Thus, a social project with an IRR of 10 percent may be considered worthwhile, but a financial project with an IRR of 10 percent may not be.

As noted above, the existence of subsidized recreation benefits for residents is one rationale for developing ecotourism programs even when the costs outweigh the financial gains from fees. However, this rationale should be made explicit and the actual benefits to residents should be quantified wherever possible through techniques such as travel cost or contingent valuation analysis.

In addition, the fact that natural areas provide both the financial ecotourism benefits and the nonfinancial traditional benefits has important implications for decisions on how much land to maintain in a natural state. First, tourism supplements traditional conservation benefits and thus increases the economic justification for conservation. Second, conservation benefits supplement tourism benefits so that conservation can still be justified even where little or no tourism potential exists.

One example of traditional benefits supplementing tourism to justify developing a national park and buffer zone is the Korup Project in Cameroon. The social benefit cost analysis of this project resulted in the data shown in Figure 4-6 (Ruitenbeek, 1989; c.f., Dixon and Sherman, 1990). Tourism generated only £1,360,000 (approximately $2,720,000 at 1992 exchange rates) in present value. Given costs of £15,239,000, tourism alone was not sufficient to justify the park project. However, when tourism benefits were combined with other benefits the park was worthwhile. Indeed, in this case tourism was vital in ensuring that benefits exceeded costs.

FUNDING SOURCES

Feasible projects may be sent out to funding agencies for review. There are a wide variety of funding sources, some of which require relatively little financial or cost benefit analysis to justify funding. Some of the more common funding sources are noted here.

Figure 4-6. Social Benefit Cost Analysis for the Korup Project
(In thousands of British pounds, base case results, 8 percent discount rate, 1989)

BENEFITS		COSTS	
DIRECT BENEFITS		**DIRECT COSTS**	
Watershed protection of fisheries	3,776	Capital costs excluding roads (1989-1995)	7,697
Sustained forest use	3,291	Capital costs of roads	1,859
Control of flood risk	1,578	Long-term operating costs (post-1995)	4,761
Tourism	1,360	Labor credit (negative cost)	(2,404)
Replaced subsistence production	997		
Soil fertility maintenance	532	**OPPORTUNITY COSTS**	
Genetic value	481	Lost forest use	2,620
		Lost stumpage value	706
INDUCED BENEFITS			
Induced cash crops	3,216	**TOTAL COSTS**	15,239
Agricultural productivity increase	905		
Induced forestry	207	**NET BENEFIT:**	1,084
		IRR TO THE PROJECT:	8.3%
TOTAL BENEFITS	16,323	**IRR TO THE COUNTRY:**	13.4%

Source: Adapted from Dixon and Sherman, 1990 (original source is Ruitenbeek, 1989).

Ecotourism projects that are financially viable may attract funding from local banks or investors. When these sources are not available, funding may often be obtained from governmental development programs, international development banks, or bilateral aid agencies. These sources often provide capital to promising private sector enterprises.

Projects that are not financially viable, but are economically viable because of the broader benefits to society, may be able to attract grants or concessionary loans from government agencies, bilateral aid agencies, or conservation organizations and foundations in industrialized countries. It is also common for national governments to provide incentives (subsidies) which may make the project financially attractive. For example, a government might provide reduced tax rates or exemption of income from taxation for a given period of time (tax holiday); distribution of government lands for tourism-related purposes, provided the majority remained in a natural and managed state; tax credits for donations of land to ecotourism/conservation projects; exemptions from import tariffs and commodity taxes; and low interest loans. Governments seeking funding for ecotourism and conservation projects can explore similar sources, such as conservation foundations, as well as sources available only to governments, such as the Global Environment Facility program administered by the World Bank.

The fund-raising campaign should outline a funding plan that will strive for self-sufficiency, be diversified, and seek long-term sources to support not only the initial and ongoing capital development costs but also the additional operational costs of specialized activities (e.g., research and travel). More innovative funding sources can also be explored, such as debt-for-nature swaps or tourism taxes.

TOURISM FEES: MANAGEMENT ISSUES

The evaluation necessary for setting fees can also inform planning for the future. An important consideration for both conservation and the tourism industry is the stability of demand for ecotourism, in general, and an individual attraction, in particular. An examination of demand factors (Figure 4-1) suggests that expected increases in population and income in source countries will lead to increased general demand for ecotourism attractions in the future. However, demand is based partly on taste, which for ecotourism is thought to be heavily dependent on public awareness and concern about the natural environment. Future ecotourism demand will depend in part on the level of concern in source countries for environmental preservation. Individual sites need to worry about the destination country's political and economic stability. There is inevitable uncertainty in forecasting future demand so caution must be used when estimating future ecotourism revenues.

Knowledge of demand factors can also help planners choose appropriate ecotourism development sites and determine priorities for improving the ecotourism product. For example, quantification of demand factors for tourism in Greece demonstrated that an increase in promotion within source countries would be a cost-effective way to increase demand by improving destination image (Papadopoulos and Witt, 1987). In the case of ecotourism, other areas for cost-effective investment might include improving the quality of the experience through guide training or development of facilities. A rigorous evaluation of the importance of respective demand factors would be useful for these purposes. In the meantime, responses to more general survey questions (such as those in Figure 4-3) can be used to prioritize opportunities for improving the ecotourism product.

TYPES OF FEES AND FEE COLLECTION

Once overall fee policies have been determined, managers must decide for what goods and services specific fees should be charged and how they should be collected. Although there is some overlap in terminology, the following are some of the common categories for fees.

Entrance fee. A fee charged to enter a park or similar attraction.

Admissions fee. A fee charged for admission to a specific facility, such as a visitor center.

Use fee. A fee for use of a specific object (for example, binoculars or snorkeling gear), service (guide), or opportunity (camping place).

License or permit. Similar to a use fee, this category includes fees such as hunting or fishing permits.

Sales and concessions. Souvenirs, lodging, and other goods and services can be sold directly by the park (with profits being considered tourism fees) or through a concessionaire agreement (with concession revenues being a kind of tourism fee).

The following are some of the common approaches to collecting fees, though alternative systems, such as annual passes, have also been suggested (Laarman and Baldares, 1990; Barborak, 1988).

Direct on-site collection. In this case, fees are collected directly from tourists, usually at an entrance gate or as the good or service is purchased. There are at least two benefits of this method: one, it directly correlates payment of fees with the service provided and two, it provides direct contact between tourists and park personnel, and thus an opportunity to inform, regulate, and count visitors.

Indirect collection through tour operators. In such a system, fees are paid by the tour operator, with the cost passed on to the tourist as part of the tour package price. This strategy is similar to direct collection, and in fact is often used as a complementary system. Although there is less contact between park personnel and visitors, this system can contribute to cooperation between the park and the local tourism industry. In addition, it will often reduce administrative costs while still allowing visitation levels to be monitored. Another benefit is that the fees are "hidden" in the cost of the tour package, thus possibly reducing the effect of higher fees on visitation levels. For example, the expensive permits for visiting the Rwandan gorillas are typically sold to tour operators rather than directly to tourists.

Indirect collection through other sectors of the tourism industry. This method, with fees usually charged through hotel or transportation taxes, provides benefits similar to tour operator fee systems. However, it is often critical for industry acceptance that fees be levied only when there is a strong correlation between the fees and park use. For example, hotels near the Tobago Cays Marine National Park in St. Vincent and the Grenadines pay a levy to help maintain the park (Rodgers, 1989), but hotels far from the park should not be asked to pay such a fee.

Additional sources of revenue should also be utilized when appropriate. For example, an opportunity should be provided for tourists, and others interested in the area, to donate funds for management of the destination. This mechanism can generate substantial revenue and may be most efficient when set up through a nongovernmental organization. For example, The Nature Conservancy solicited $150,000 for the Darwin Research Station in the Galápagos by mailing an appeal for donations to tourists who had signed the station's guest log (Warner, 1989). A recent survey of tour operators suggests that 63 percent of ecotourists would be willing to donate $50 toward conserving the area they visit; 27 percent would pay $200.

The best fee system for any particular area will be based on the type of visitation (individuals versus groups), the level of cooperation with the industry, bureaucratic efficiency, and other relevant factors. For, example, managers can use a combination of fees to allow different groups to pay for the specific services which they receive. Charging a low entrance fee and a relatively high guide fee may generate substantial revenue from wealthy tourists interested in hiring guides while at the same time maintaining visits by less wealthy tourists who may be more likely to frequent local tourism businesses, which thereby support the local economy. However, the number of different fees should be kept to a minimum to avoid tourist confusion and frustration.

Regardless of what system is implemented, tour operators should be notified far in advance (one year is often suggested) about changes in the type or size of fees so they can adjust their prices accordingly. In addition, efforts to inform visitors of the importance of fee revenue for park management usually increases their support for such fees.

SOME GENERAL PRINCIPLES FOR TOURISM FEE POLICY

The above discussion illustrates specific objectives and methods regarding tourism fees. However, in framing entrance fee policy, some general principles should be considered.

View tourism fees as a supplement to, rather than replacement for, existing budgets. One of the main rationales for developing ecotourism is that it can provide much needed funding for conservation budgets. If existing budgets are reduced as tourism revenues increase, there is little benefit from ecotourism. Indeed, the infrastructural and management costs brought on by the introduction or expansion of visitation may actually reduce funding available for traditional management activities. The instability of tourism revenues may also be worse than the instability of existing government funding. Whenever possible, establish trust funds to ensure continued funding during low points in tourism cycles.

Earmark at least a portion of tourism revenues back into the parks which generate them. Experience in the United States and elsewhere demonstrates that earmarking increases managerial efficiency in fee collection as well as responsibility in expenditure.

Establish national guidelines for fees, but set fees on a decentralized and site-specific basis. National policies, such as choosing between cost recovery and profit maximization objectives, should be developed for fees charged at government attractions. However, managers of individual parks should have flexibility in setting fees based on specific local resource conditions as well as changes in demand for the attraction. If the decisions remain with the central government, the authority to change fees should at least remain as flexible as possible. For example, the executive branch, such as a parks agency, can generally respond more quickly than can the legislative branch, such as a parliament or congress (Barborak, 1988).

Recognize that fee collection will not be worthwhile at all attractions. Fee collection may simply not be cost-effective at sites with low levels of demand or high administrative costs.

Develop and maintain accurate accounting and financial management systems for both revenues and expenditures. Informed decisions on fee levels require knowledge of both the cost of providing the tourism opportunity and the revenue generated through fees. Efficient decisions can only be made when such information is systematically collected and incorporated into the decision making process. When possible, this accounting should be supplemented by information on ecologic and social impacts.

USING ECOTOURISM TO SUPPORT ECONOMIC DEVELOPMENT

Ecotourism has been embraced by many as an opportunity to generate income and employment in areas relatively untouched by traditional development efforts. Such goals have often been achieved in part, but there is a realization that little of the money spent by tourists remains at or near the destination itself (Lindberg, 1991; Boo, 1990).

There are at least three reasons for increasing local benefits from, and participation in, ecotourism development. First, it is equitable insofar as conservation of the area for ecotourism reduces or eliminates traditional resource utilization. Second, when residents receive benefits they usually support ecotourism, even to the point of protecting the site against poaching or other encroachment. Conversely, if residents bear the costs without receiving benefits they often turn against ecotourism and might intentionally or unintentionally damage the attraction. Third, the ecotourists, as consumers, often support the importance of tourism benefitting local residents (Eagles, Ballantine, and Fennell, 1992).

This section discusses principles and mechanisms for increasing ecotourism's contribution to local economic development. For a broader discussion of ecotourism's role in sustainable development, see Healy (1991).

The amount of money which actually reaches the destination region, less the amount leaked out to pay for outside goods and services, has not been adequately quantified. However, a common estimate is that less than 10 percent of tourist spending remains in communities near ecotourism destinations. To some extent, this is simply due to the nature of the tourism industry; substantial funds are spent on marketing and transport before tourists even reach the destination. However, there are opportunities for expanding ecotourism's local economic benefits. Many of these are currently being pursued by privately or publicly funded programs. As these programs progress, we should be able to determine which are most effective in achieving economic development goals.

Some of the mechanisms for increasing local benefits from ecotourism include: local ownership and management of the ecotourism resource; leasing, partial ownership, or profit sharing arrangements between the tourism industry and local residents; direct payments to communities from tourism revenues; and local employment in the tourism industry. In practice, the most appropriate mechanism, or group of mechanisms, will depend on local cultural, political, and economic conditions. The following examples illustrate some of what has been done.

EXAMPLE 1: LOCAL OWNERSHIP IN ZIMBABWE

In the 1980s, Zimbabwe developed the Communal Areas Management Programme For Indigenous Resources (CAMPFIRE) model, under which district councils have been granted "appropriate authority" to manage wildlife within their region (Heath, 1992; Murindagomo, 1990). Significantly, the Ministry of Natural Resources and Tourism has required that district councils demonstrate endorsement by its membership and the ability to implement a wildlife management plan as a prerequisite to receiving this authority.

Where this has occurred, CAMPFIRE has enabled district councils to directly manage, and profit from, hunting, photography tourism, and other forms of wildlife utilization. In the Guruve district, for example, the 1989 hunting season generated Z$61,340 (approximately $24,536) in dividends to wards, with an additional $195,315 available for equipment purchase, funding for the district council, and other purposes. The Kanyurira ward received $18,924, of which the majority was earmarked for community projects and direct payments to households of $80 each. In comparison, the average household in the area earned $200 from cotton during the same period (Murindagomo, 1990).

EXAMPLE 2: DIRECT PAYMENT AND EMPLOYMENT GENERATION IN ZAMBIA

As noted in the section on fees, the Lupande Development Project near the South Luangwa National Park provides for hunting and other wildlife utilization benefits being channeled back into wildlife management and local communities through the Wildlife Conservation Revolving Fund (Lewis, Kaweche, and Mwenya, 1990). Forty percent of these funds are given to local chiefs for community projects; in 1986 this equalled $7,950.

In addition to the direct financial benefits, 114 local residents were actively employed in the conservation programs, hunting operations, and hippopotamus harvests. This contribution to local employment demonstrates how ecotourism can support rural economic development. Because employment engenders local support for the conservation programs that have generated the jobs, ecotourism also contributes to conservation. Indeed, poaching of elephants and black rhinos, which had been significantly increasing, decreased at least tenfold between 1985 and 1987.

EXAMPLE 3: DIRECT PAYMENT IN KENYA

Kenya has long been a leading money earner in the ecotourism field, and revenues are expected to expand further as higher fee levels are implemented. Revenue from public parks and reserves is projected to increase from $23.6 million in 1990 to $53.7 million in 1995 (constant 1990 dollars) (Kenya Wildlife Service, 1990).

One of Kenya's priorities is to share 25 percent of entrance fee revenue with communities bordering the protected areas. This program is explicitly designed to reimburse communities for the direct and indirect costs associated with establishing the protected area. Distribution of funds will be based on costs incurred, such as loss of crops and cattle to wildlife.

These examples involve the relatively profitable activities of African game hunting and viewing. However, the concept is valid elsewhere. For example, the Annapurna Conservation Area Project (ACAP) in Nepal annually generates $200,000 from trekking fees to fund ACAP activities and community projects (Wells, 1992). The $3.50 entrance fee at the Tavoro Forest Park and Reserve in Fiji generated $8,000 in revenues between March and November of 1991. Of this total, approximately half was used to pay salaries and expenses and half was used for community development projects (Young, 1992).

INCREASING ECONOMIC DEVELOPMENT BY REDUCING LEAKAGE AND IMPROVING LINKAGES

Perhaps the most obvious opportunity for providing local benefits is employing local residents in the tourism industry and the industries which support it. The money spent by tourists is circulated through the economy as the tourism sector and its employees buy goods from other businesses. Thus, tourism might support not only a local lodge manager but also a local farmer who grows the food sold in the lodge. On the other hand, if the local lodge imports its food, the money "leaks" away and produces fewer local benefits. To increase local development, tourism should be "linked" to other sectors so that money helps develop the local economy rather than being leaked away (what constitutes the "local" economy depends on the region of interest; it might be a village, a province, or some other unit). The following paragraphs illustrate opportunities for reducing the leakage of tourism revenue.

Improve linkages within the tourism industry. Perhaps the most obvious opportunity for local residents to benefit from ecotourism is through employment and income in the industry itself. In the short term, this employment may center on unskilled labor. However, training programs should be developed so that residents are able to fill skilled positions, such as guides and managers. In addition, financing should be made available for local entrepreneurs to establish their own tourism operations.

Improve linkages to the local transportation industry. Ecotourists often need to, and want to, use existing local modes of transportation, ranging from the traditional to the modern. Whenever possible, local boats, canoes, mules, taxis, and porters should be utilized. In some cases, cooperatives can be formed to purchase more expensive transportation equipment. For example, the boats that carry tourists from Puno to Taquile on Lake Titicaca in Peru are owned by a local cooperative.

Improve linkages with agriculture and fishing. Substantial tourism expenditures go toward purchasing food, much of which is currently imported from regions distant from actual tourism attractions (Miller, 1985). Ecotourists tend to be interested in local cuisine, provided that quality standards are met and maintained. Lodges and restaurants often need to be more willing to spend the extra time developing local sources of food. Meanwhile, local farmers and distributors often need to recognize the importance of quality and reliability.

Improve linkages with construction, equipment, and maintenance sectors. Because ecotourism infrastructure is typically small-scale and located in remote locations, local labor and materials are often employed in its construction. This linkage should be maintained and expanded.

Develop local handicrafts and other souvenirs. Souvenir sales are often the easiest way for local residents to benefit from tourism spending, but many destinations sell souvenirs from other regions or even other countries. Instead, a commitment should be made to developing local handicrafts while considering what is appealing to tourists.

How will local benefits from ecotourism be maximized? Using the simple example of a lodge, the goal would be to: develop tourism that maximizes spending at the lodge (increase gross revenues); develop programs that promote local owner-ship and management of the lodge (increase direct benefits for each dollar of gross revenue); and develop strong links between the lodge and local farmers, and fund programs to help farmers provide products which the lodge still imports from outside the region (reduce leakage and increase indirect benefits).

To some extent, these linkages will develop spontaneously to meet imme-diate needs. However, active involvement by community leaders, industry, government officials, and nongovernmental organizations will often be necessary. For example, the industry can work with local communities to identify opportunities for employment in the industry or for providing goods such as food and handicrafts. The government can often play a vital role in providing credit to entrepreneurs or training through extension programs. Nongovernmental organizations can play important roles in training and other activities. These varied groups will need to cooperate in order to: identify opportunities for local development; identify training, credit, and other programs necessary for realistically achieving these opportunities; implement these programs; and evaluate program successes and failures, trying new strategies where appropriate.

EMPLOYMENT AND TRAINING APPROACHES

One example of such cooperation to increase employment is the guide training program developed by the La Selva Biological Station with funding from World Wildlife Fund and in cooperation with the Costa Rican National Parks Service and other organizations (Paaby, Clark and González, 1991). A group of twenty-six local residents (selected from ninety-three applicants) participated in forty hours of lectures and 103 hours of guided field walks, which covered topics ranging from general ecology to bird-watching techniques.

Although this program was not intended to substitute for a full degree in interpretation (for example, most participants did not have foreign language skills), the results have been positive. The guides formed a local cooperative (Natucoop) and were successful in finding employment on both a part- and full-time basis.

Training programs have also been implemented to develop reliable and high quality food sources, improve sanitation standards, and more. In Bali, Indonesia, an experimental farm was established to improve the quality and variety of fruits, vegetables, and poultry products for sale to tourist hotels and restaurants. An important component of this program focused on marketing, including organizing a reliable supply of products (Inskeep, 1991). Meanwhile, Kenya reduced its food imports from 77 percent of tourist food consumption in 1984 to 14 percent in 1988 (Dieke, 1991).

Nepal's Annapurna Conservation Area Project (ACAP) not only channeled entrance fees back into the local region but also included training to upgrade service quality, standardize menus and prices, and improve sanitation and waste disposal standards (Wells, 1992). Some staff training programs may be developed with public funding, while others may be provided by the private sector as part of a license agreement permitting establishment of tourism businesses (Ankomah and Crompton, 1990, note such arrangements in several countries). A variety of training programs are described by Inskeep (1991).

Economic development programs such as training and provision of rural credit have faced a variety of roadblocks, and many have failed or only partially succeeded. Some difficulties include inappropriate project design or implementation, limited resident skills and experience with outsiders, and conflict over income distribution. It is clear that developing programs which successfully train local residents, disburse credit, and attain related economic development goals are some of the most important challenges currently facing ecotourism.

In addition, decisions on which programs to pursue will often need to be prioritized in light of limited human and financial resources. Should priority be given to providing training for local guides or for developing local agricultural inputs? Is it more important to develop an "up-market" program, thus attracting tourists who might spend more but require more imports, or to develop "backpacker" ecotourism which might generate less gross revenue but be more easily linked to the local economy and possibly cause less ecologic damage in the park?

These questions can be answered in part through multiplier analysis, a measure of how tourism (or any industry) is linked to other sectors of the economy. Multipliers have often been misunderstood and misused (Eadington and Redman, 1991; Archer, 1984). And as they are currently employed multipliers are more useful in comparing industries than comparing different types of tourism development or identifying opportunities to improve linkages. Furthermore, the data necessary for calculating multipliers is often unavailable or of questionable accuracy.

However, the basic multiplier concept is useful, and valuable information can be obtained from surveying the ecotourism businesses about their employment and purchasing patterns; that is, by identifying their linkage with the local economy (Milne, 1992; Borge et al., 1990). Analysis of the responses helps planners determine which types of tourism development, such as backpackers versus up-market, best meets income or employment goals. In addition, it can be used to identify those sectors—agricultural inputs, for example—which can be developed to increase linkages and thus increase the amount of money retained by the local economy.

When a full multiplier analysis is not possible, similar information can still be obtained by a less rigorous examination of how money flows through the ecotourism industry. Community leaders could, informally or formally, interview tourism businesses to identify where money leaks away from the local economy (in many cases, leakage will be obvious and interviews will be unnecessary). This information can then be used to prioritize programs that will reduce this leakage and thus improve local benefits. If surveys of tourism businesses demonstrate that most guides are hired in the capital city, but most food consumed by the tourists is from the local area, the priority will be to develop programs to train local residents as guides.

However, if most of the food is imported from other regions or countries, then a decision may have to be made between allocating funds for training guides or for developing agricultural products for the tourism market. The business surveys could be used to determine which option would produce more jobs. Depending on priorities, the decision on which project to fund might be based on the following considerations:

- how much each project costs and to what extent it will achieve its objective (Will the agricultural products truly be acceptable? Will the guides be adequately trained?);

- how many jobs will be created;

- the desirability of these jobs (Will guiding jobs be more desirable than agriculture?); and

- the stablility of the jobs (Can the agricultural or handicraft products be sold if tourism declines?).

INCREASING TOURIST SPENDING IN THE LOCAL ECONOMY

The converse of reducing leakage is increasing tourist spending. Studies in Latin America and Thailand suggest that additional revenues can be earned by developing infrastructure and services at or near ecotourism attractions (Boo, 1990; Dixon and Sherman, 1990). These might include lodging, restaurants or snack bars, souvenir shops, visitor centers, cultural performances, and so on. Figure 4-7 (an extension of Figure 4-3) includes sample questions for surveys that will help identify opportunities for increasing tourism spending and reducing leakage out of the economy. These surveys can also include questions concerning current spending patterns, thereby identifying current direct economic impact on local communities (in general, tourists will be best able to identify the impact of their spending when traveling as individuals rather than as prepaid tour groups).

Careful planning is particularly important when developing these additional facilities. It may be best to locate infrastructure outside the park, thus reducing negative ecological impacts while increasing opportunities for local residents to participate in the tourism economy. However, locating facilities in villages may increase negative social and cultural impacts, while at the same time foregoing the park's ability to regulate ecological impacts.

Care should be taken to avoid indirect damage to the local environment, culture, or economy. Handicrafts should not be based on consumption of flora or fauna when this consumption will endanger the species or local customs. Coral and bird feather souvenirs are often cited as examples of how handicraft production can cause severe damage to natural resources.

Throughout the planning process, consideration should be given both to local cultural and economic traditions and to tourists' tastes and desires. For example, in some cases crafts cooperatives will be culturally appropriate (and appealing to tourists) while in other cases individual vendors will be appropriate.

Figure 4-7. Sample Survey Questions for Identifying Opportunities to Increase Tourism Spending and Reduce Leakage

If we developed lodging or restaurant facilities here would you use them?

Definitely ❑   Probably ❑   Unlikely ❑   No ❑

What type of facilities would you prefer?

High quality and expensive ❑   Average quality and price ❑
Basic and inexpensive ❑

Did you purchase any souvenirs during your trip? If yes, can you give us an approximation of how much they cost?

If we expanded our selection of souvenirs, would you buy more?

What kinds of souvenirs are you most interested in?

1. Local crafts; what types?_____
2. Books and other information materials.
3. T-shirts and other clothing.
4. Other items; please list :_____

Did you eat food which, as far as you could tell, was special to this region?
Yes ❑   No ❑   If not, why not?

   1. It was not offered to me.
   2. I was concerned about the quality of the food.
   3. I did not like the taste of local food.

If we were to develop XX, would you be interested and willing to pay to participate in this activity? (XX could be a supplemental activity such as a visitor center, a cultural performance, etc.)

Tourism also puts new demands on local economies, particularly those in remote areas. Consumption of local products can be an important benefit of ecotourism, but this demand should be managed carefully so it does not shock local economies or the local environment. For example, tourist demand for firewood in Nepal has increased the cost of wood to the Nepalese as well as caused severe deforestation. There are often opportunities for reducing these shocks; the Annapurna Conservation Area Project (ACAP) now requires that trekkers use kerosene rather than firewood.

CONCLUSION

Ecotourism has attracted substantial attention based on its ability to provide economic benefits to conservation and rural development. In many regions ecotourism has made vital contributions in both fields. However, this attention has also revealed that much still needs to be done. This chapter has presented and illustrated several strategies for managing ecotourism such that its benefits are maintained and, hopefully, expanded.

REFERENCES

Alderman, C. 1990. "A Study of the Role of Privately Owned Lands Used for Nature Tourism, Education, and Conservation." Paper prepared for the Yale School of Forestry and Conservation International (May).

Ankomah, P. K. and J. L. Crompton. 1990. "Unrealized Tourism Potential: The Case of Sub-Saharan Africa." *Tourism Management*, vol. 11, pp. 11–28.

Anonymous. 1992. "Through the Roof." *The Economist*. August 1, p. 32.

Archer, B. H. 1984. "Economic Impact: Misleading Multiplier." *Annals of Tourism Research*, vol. 11, no. 3, pp. 517–18.

Ashton, R. E., and L. Haysmith. 1992. *Handbook on Central American Tourism and Conservation*. Bronx, N.Y.: Wildlife Conservation International Paseo Pantera Ecotourism Program, USAID RENARM Project.

Aukerman, R. 1990. *User Pays for Recreation Resources*. Fort Collins, Colo.: Colorado State University Research Services.

Baldares, M. J. and J. G. Laarman. 1990. *User Fees at Protected Areas in Costa Rica*. Research Triangle Park, N.C.: Forestry Private Enterprise Initiative Working Paper No. 48.

Bamford, T. E., R. E. Manning, L. K. Forcier, and E. J. Koenemann. 1988. "Differential Campsite Pricing: An Experiment." *Journal of Leisure Research*, vol. 20, no. 4, pp. 324–42.

Barborak, J. R. 1988. "Innovative Funding Mechanisms Used by Costa Rican Conservation Agencies." Paper presented at the IUCN General Assembly, San Jose, Costa Rica (February).

Boo, E. 1990. *Ecotourism: Potential and Pitfalls.* Washington, D.C.: World Wildlife Fund.

Borge, L., et al. 1990. *Ecotonomic Impact of Wildlife-Based Tourism in Northern Botswana.* Fargo, N.D.: North Dakota State University.

Bovaird, A. G., M. J. Tricker, and R. Stoakes. 1984. *Recreation Management and Pricing: The Effect of Charging Policy on Demand at Countryside Recreation Sites.* Aldershot, U.K.: Gower Publishing Company.

Brealey, R. A., and S. C. Myers. 1988. *Principles of Corporate Finance*, third ed. New York: McGraw-Hill.

Child, G. F. T. and R. A. Heath. 1990. "Underselling National Parks in Zimbabwe: The Implications for Rural Sustainability." *Society and Natural Resources*, vol. 3, pp. 215–27.

Dieke, P. U. C. 1991. "Policies for Tourism Development in Kenya." *Annals of Tourism Research*, vol. 18, no. 2, pp. 269–94.

Dixon, J. and P. Sherman. 1990. *Economics of Protected Areas: A New Look at Benefits and Costs.* Washington, D.C.: Island Press.

Durojaiye, B., and A. Ikpi. 1988. "The Monetary Value of Recreation Facilities in a Developing Economy: A Case Study of Three Centers in Nigeria." *Natural Resources Journal*, vol. 28, no. 2, pp. 315–28.

Eadington, W. R., and M. Redman. 1991. "Economics and Tourism." *Annals of Tourism Research*, vol. 18, no. 1, pp. 41–56.

Eagles, P. F. J., J. L. Ballantine, and D. A. Fennell. 1992. "Marketing to the Ecotourist: Case Studies From Kenya and Costa Rica." Mimeo, Dept. of Recreation and Leisure Studies, University of Waterloo, Ontario, Canada.

Economist Intelligence Unit (EIU). 1991. "Kenya," *EIU International Tourism Reports*, no. 2., pp. 49–66.

Edwards, S. F. 1987. *An Introduction to Coastal Zone Economics: Concepts, Methods and Case Studies.* New York: Taylor & Francis.

Gurung, H. 1990. "Environmental Management of Mountain Tourism in Nepal." Paper presented at ESCAP Symposium on Tourism Promotion in the Asia Region, Hangzhou, China.

Healy, R. 1991. "The Role of Tourism in Sustainable Development." Unpublished manuscript. Durham, N.C.: Duke University School of the Environment.

Heath, R. 1992. "The Growth of Wildlife Based Tourism in Zimbabwe." Paper presented at the IUCN IV World Congress on National Parks and Protected Areas, Caracas, Venezuela (February).

Henry, W., J. Waithaka, and C. G. Gakahu. 1992. "Visitor Attitudes, Perceptions, Norms and Use Patterns Influencing Visitor Carrying Capacity," in C. G. Gakahu, ed. *Tourist Attitudes and Use Impacts in Maasai Mara National Reserve*. Nairobi, Kenya: Wildlife Conservation International.

Henry, W. and D. Western. 1988. "Tourism and Conservation in Kenya's National Parks: Planning for a Better Partnership," in E. E. Krumpe and P. D. Weingart, eds. *Management of Park and Wilderness Reserves: Proceedings of a Symposium at the 4th World Wilderness Congress*. Moscow, Idaho: Wilderness Research Center.

Huber, R. M., and W. Park. 1991. *Development Plan and Financial Analysis for the Enhancement of the Sulphur Springs Natural Landmark*. Feasibility Report, OAS/St. Lucia Tourist Board. St. Lucia: Voice Press.

Inskeep, E. 1991. *Tourism Planning: An Integrated and Sustainable Development Approach*. New York: Van Nostrand Reinhold.

Kenya Wildlife Service. 1990. "A Policy Framework and Development Programme 1991-1996." Nairobi, Kenya: Kenya Wildlife Service (November).

Laarman, J. G., and M. J. Baldares. 1990. *Demand for an Annual Pass to Costa Rica's National Parks*. FPEI Working Paper No. 47. Research Triangle Park, N.C.: Southeastern Center for Forest Economics Research.

Leakey, R. 1990. Lecture at the Smithsonian Institution, Washington, D.C. (October).

Lewis, D., G. B. Kaweche, and A. Mwenya. 1990. "Wildlife Conservation Outside Protected Areas—Lessons from an Experiment in Zambia." *Conservation Biology*, vol. 4, no. 2, pp. 171–80.

Lindberg, K. 1991. *Policies for Maximizing Nature Tourism's Ecological and Economic Benefits*. Washington, D.C.: World Resources Institute.

McNeely, J. 1988. *Economics and Biological Diversity: Developing and Using Economic Incentives to Conserve Biological Resources*. Gland, Switzerland: IUCN.

Miller, L. 1985. "Linking Tourism and Agriculture to Create Jobs and Reduce Migration in the Caribbean," in R. A. Paster, ed. *Migration and Development in the Caribbean: The Unexplored Connection*. Boulder, Colo.: Westview Press.

Milne, S. 1992. "Tourism and Economic Development in South Pacific Island Microstates." *Annals of Tourism Research*, vol. 19, no. 2, pp. 191–212.

Ministere de Plan (Republique Rwandaise). 1989. *Strategie Nationale de L'environnement au Rwanda, Volume 1*. Diagnostic, Version Provisoire (October).

Murindagomo, F. 1990. "Zimbabwe: Windfall and Campfire," in A. Kiss, ed. *Living with Wildlife: Wildlife Resource Management with Local Participation in Africa*. Washington, D.C.: World Bank, Technical Paper Number 130.

Noland, D. 1992. "Upping the Trekker's Ante." *Outside*, April, pp. 140, 142.

Olindo, P. 1991. "The Old Man of Nature Tourism: Kenya," in T. Whelan, ed. *Nature Tourism: Managing for the Environment.* Washington, D.C.: Island Press.

Paaby. P., D. B. Clark, and H. González. 1991. "Training Rural Residents as Naturalist Guides: Evaluation of a Pilot Project in Costa Rica." *Conservation Biology*, vol. 5, no. 4, pp. 542–46.

Papadopoulos, S. I., and S. F. Witt. 1985. "A Marketing Analysis of Foreign Tourism in Greece," in S. Shaw, L. Sparks, and E. Kaynak, eds. *Proceedings of Second World Marketing Congress.* Stirling, U.K.: University of Stirling.

Rodgers, K. 1989. Speech at the "Miami Conference on the Caribbean" (November).

Rosenthal, D. H., J. B. Loomis, and G. L. Peterson. 1984. "Pricing for Efficiency and Revenue in Public Recreation Areas." *Journal of Leisure Research*, vol. 16, no. 3, pp. 195–208.

Ruitenbeek, H. J. 1989. *Social Cost-Benefit Analysis of the Korup Project, Cameroon.* London: World Wide Fund for Nature.

Smith, S. L. J. 1989. *Tourism Analysis: A Handbook.* New York: John Wiley & Sons.

Tobias, D. and R. Mendelsohn. 1991. "Valuing Ecotourism in a Tropical Rain-Forest Reserve." *Ambio*, vol. 20, no. 2, pp. 91–93.

Vedder, A. and W. Weber. 1990. "Rwanda: The Mountain Gorilla Project (Volcanoes National Park)," in A. Kiss, ed. *Living with Wildlife: Wildlife Resource Management with Local Participation in Africa.* Washington, D.C.: World Bank Technical Paper Number 130.

Walsh, R. G. 1986. *Recreation Economic Decisions: Comparing Benefits and Costs.* State College, Penn.: Venture Publishing.

Warner, E. 1989. "Ecotourism!" *Environmental Action*, September/October, p. 21.

Wells, M. P. 1992. "Economic Benefits and Costs of Protected Areas in Nepal." Paper presented at the IUCN IV World Congress on National Parks and Protected Areas. Caracas, Venezuela (February).

Young, M. 1992. "People and Parks—Factor for the Success of Community Based Ecotourism in the Conservation of Tropical Rainforest." Paper presented at the IUCN IV World Congress on National Parks and Protected Areas. Caracas, Venezuela (February).

A Window to the Natural World: The Design of Ecotourism Facilities

David L. Andersen

Ths chapter focuses on the design, development, and operation of facilities that embody the general principles of environmentally sensitive design and sustainable development. The issues discussed will, in many cases, transcend purely architectural and development issues. This is a reflection of the complexities of the ecotourism experience and the need to involve the conservation of the environment and local culture. This writer views the facility as a "window to the natural world" and as a vehicle for learning and understanding. Though it is just one component in the ecotourism formula, the design of the facility can reinforce and enhance the ecotourist's enjoyment and understanding of the setting. Providing comfortable lodging with low ecological impact is key to the success of an ecotourism facility, but such facilities should also serve as windows to the natural world and as vehicles for learning and understanding.

FACILITIES SEARCHING FOR DEFINITION AND ETHICAL STANDARDS

As the fringes of the last wilderness areas are besieged by lumbering and often inappropriate agricultural techniques, ecotourism facilities, field stations, and environmental learning centers are crowding in for the opportunity to appreciate these unique wilderness areas. Currently ecotourism represents a small but growing niche in a global tourism marketplace. Detailed information on specific facilities is available in the book *Rainforest: A Guide to Research and Tourist Facilities* (Castner, 1990). Although it is a comprehensive review of facilities in place at the time of its publication, the recent explosive growth in ecotourism facilities has outpaced efforts to catalog them.

The growth of this market niche has been limited by lack of facilities and general lack of supporting infrastructure for tourism. To continue the growth of ecotourism as an industry it is important for governments and private enterprise to pool technical, cultural, and financial resources to carry out a meaningful environmental agenda. Governments and local communities must have the wisdom, foresight, and political courage to view ecotourism as a limited-growth opportunity and not as unbridled development that strangles the environment. The challenge ahead is to build a few good facilities firmly founded in the understanding that tourism should not be a singular industry on which a community relies for economic support. Although ecotourism may be seen by some as a savior for economically depressed areas, it must be part of a balanced long-term economic plan involving other sustainable industries.

Outside of ecotourism there are other encouraging developments in the tourism industry. Major hotel chains such as Marriott Corporation are experimenting with "environmentally-sound rooms," i.e., utilizing materials and construction techniques that result in low environmental impact. Choice Hotels are providing recycling containers in rooms and encouraging conservation by their guests. These "environmentally friendly" activities in no way equate with ecotourism, but they do illustrate the potential for the ecotourism facility concept to influence mainstream hospitality design.

Some countries, such as Belize, Costa Rica, Ecuador, and Venezuela, may have a comparative advantage in the development of ecotourism because of their existing governmental policies and infrastructure. Though many other countries currently lack policies and infrastructure, they also have opportunities to develop their ecotourism industries more thoughtfully by learning from the experience of the more advanced ecotourism industries. Costa Rica, for example, is experiencing some success with ecotourism, but it is also struggling to come to grips with the capacity of the environment to sustain Costa Rica's sudden popularity as a tourist destination. Similarly, Papua New Guinea has much potential for ecotourism, but can the culture of perhaps the world's last stone axmakers survive increasing encounters with outsiders? What will be the effect on the family traditions and crafts of the native population of Papua New Guinea's Trobriand Islands as boatloads of tourists arrive? Obviously these questions are larger than the tourism industry, but the developer of ecotourism facilities must be aware of cultural and economic effects on the native population while planning facilities in such areas.

The sensitivity of designs for the built environment on nature's fragile edge will have an important impact on the conservation efforts embodied in ecotourism and scientific and educational ventures. Establishment of environmental codes of ethics and general design criteria for ecotourism are positive steps towards implementation of this sensitivity. There is much interest in wilderness conservation and the ecotourism facility can do much to set the stage for conservation. The ecotourism developer, however, is only one actor in this real life drama.

FINANCIAL ISSUES IN BUILDING FACILITIES

It may be that ecotourism is a way for some communities and individuals to make a living from the task of saving our planet. To date, unfortunately, many so-called ecotourism facilities have been rude intrusions on the landscape. It has been easy to rationalize the design (or lack thereof) and construction of these facilities based on the limited budgets of nonprofit entities that are often involved in the development of educational and scientific facilities. Similarly, their for-profit colleagues in ecotourism typically have limited budgets as well. In fact, budget constraints rarely allow competent design professionals to participate in such projects.

The limited size of a typical ecotourism facility precludes the participation of major hospitality corporations. To date, ecotourism has been the domain of small-scale developers. Limited resources have often generated poor planning and design of facilities, but have also resulted in a wide variety of design responses. The typical hands-on approach to management of ecotourism facilities is perhaps the best assurance that these operations can be responsive to changing conditions in the natural environment to which they provide access. To their credit, these same operators have created some unique "hands-on architecture."

There is, however, increasing interest in ecotourism by major hoteliers. The economics of resort operation seem to be directing the ecotourism marketplace towards larger facilities. Traditional first-class hotels require a minimum of fifty rooms to offset staff and infrastructure costs. By comparison a small-scale owner/operator may be able to survive economically with as few as twelve to twenty units (or less) depending on the local economy. The ultimate size of a facility must not exceed the ability of the environment to sustain it (National Park Service, 1992). The challenge that lies ahead is to find a way for larger tourist operations to participate in such projects. However, the efforts by Marriott Corporation and Choice Hotels to develop ecologically sensitive lodging in the mass tourism industry demonstrate that ecologic sensitivity can be a wise business decision.

Although the limited size of ecotourism facilities generally precludes the participation of major hospitality corporations, small operations can also be ecologically sensitive. One approach may be the development of strategic alliances between large urban or beachfront hotels and small-scale ecotourism facilities. This satellite relationship with larger hotels may benefit both the ecotourism operator with a steady flow of guests and the larger hotel with the possibility of extended and/or repeat stays by guests. Such innovative strategies may be crucial to ensure that ecotourism does not excessively stress the environment which serves as the primary attraction.

Major financing agencies, such as the World Bank or the International Environmental Investment Fund of the U.S. Overseas Private Investment Corporation (OPIC), are increasingly funding ecotourism infrastructure. These agencies typically seek large projects, so strategies, such as satellite development, need to be developed which combine large funding opportunities with limited ecologic impact.

ORGANIZATIONAL ISSUES

As one looks toward a particular region for the development of ecotourism facilities, there are a number of broadly conceptual issues to address.

- Is the area so unique that it requires government protection?

- Is the infrastructure sufficient to support ecotourism?

- Has an analysis been done of the area's ecologic sensitivity?

- Is the facility development for *current* market demand or does it anticipate *future* market demand? Is phased development possible?

- Will the facility offer a variety of choices for lodging in the area? Variety offers tourists the opportunity for an extended stay in an area and the anticipation of return visits. Lodging-type variety will also give the area exposure to a greater cross-section of the market.

- How can the facility express the unique characteristics of an area and its people? Encourage and facilitate the participation and advice of the native people and tour operators in the area.

- How can the region profit from common marketing channels for all facilities in the area?

- What are the expectations of the visitor for lodging facilities in the area?

Upon securing a potential building site the developer should anticipate the following:

- Obtaining a boundary survey and posting the perimeter.

- Obtaining a topographic survey with the appropriate contour intervals identified for detailed study.

- Locating significant site features, trees, marshes, streams, existing structures (if any), archaeologically significant areas, etc.

- Obtaining aerial photographs of the site to confirm survey information.

- Identifying seasonal high-water marks.

- Investigating approval requirements by local and national agencies.

- Identifying sustainable power sources on the site.

- Identifying seismic zone classification.

- Investigation of soil conditions and bearing capacities for building.

- Observing prevailing winds and weather patterns as they affect the site during *all* seasons.

- Reviewing the local watershed layout relative to the site, noting activities on adjacent property which may impact drainage and water quality.

- Investigating present and planned uses of adjacent property.

- Investigating site history if it has been previously occupied by man.

- Studying any significant archaeological sites on the property.

- Studying local building technologies.

- Surveying the availability of skilled and unskilled craftsmen.

- Identifying sources of building materials and the methods of transport to the site to minimize use of imported materials wherever possible.

Looking for Clues in the Environment

One component missing from many existing ecotourism facilities is a sense of fantasy, adventure, and discovery. Although most visitors come to these attractions for the beauty and uniqueness of the natural environment, many tourists also have very civilized expectations regarding lodging facilities. I do not advocate creation of a theme park atmosphere or overly plush getaway suites, but it is important to address the pragmatic requirements for basic shelter. Lodging should have a vibrant and engaging design that fulfills the expectations of the tourist who has come to be immersed in a unique wild setting and yet enjoys a few creature comforts at the end of the day.

The expectations of ecotourists cannot be easily identified or quantified. It is a diverse market and ecotourists have a variety of motivations and needs. Though some ecotourists may be quite happy with tent structures, others will prefer (and pay for) enclosed rooms with private baths and other amenities. Facilities and infrastructure need to respond to actual and expected needs.

Nature is the obvious source of inspiration for the architectural design of ecotourism facilities. (See Figure 5-1.) Unfortunately, many recently built facilities take design inspiration from crowded cities where real estate markets and manufactured building materials dictate form, color, and ambience which are foreign to the

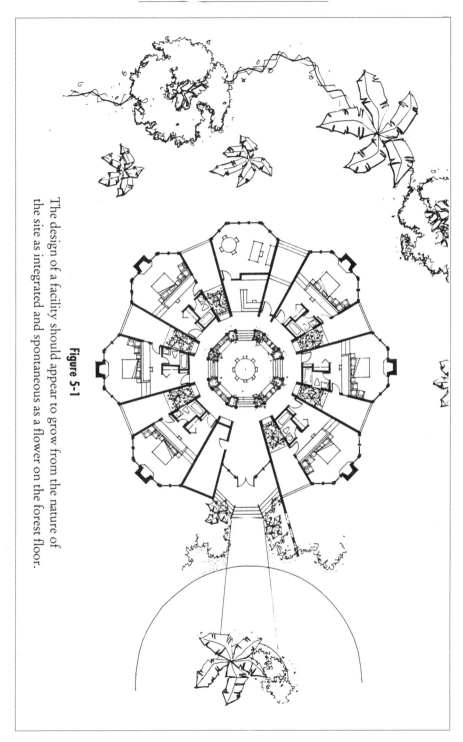

Figure 5-1

The design of a facility should appear to grow from the nature of the site as integrated and spontaneous as a flower on the forest floor.

pristine settings of ecotourism facilities. Many are both out of touch with nature and the building skills of local tradespeople, as well as being perceived by the visitor as ordinary and uninspiring.

Just as late architect Frank Lloyd Wright promoted an organic architecture for mainstream development (Wright, 1954), designers and developers must take a fresh view at opportunities to create organic architectural formats that appear to grow from the unique nature of each site, as integrated and spontaneous as a flower on the forest floor. The architecture must go beyond the requirements of shelter to be an outgrowth of the setting and a unique embodiment of provisions for guest needs and comfort.

Ecotourism as a phenomenon departs from the traditional tourism formula of sea, sun, and sand. It represents an adventure, a learning opportunity, conservation, and a spiritual experience within nature. To fully realize these objectives the facility must also depart from traditional formulae.

The setting is the best source of inspiration for the design of ecotourism facilities. The forms of living plants, trees, and the configuration of the land itself are a rich library of architectural structures. These forms have evolved over millions of years and represent time-tested successes for efficiency, function, and beauty.

In order to draw closer to nature and begin to understand its complexities, one must abandon the shapes, textures, and surfaces of manufactured products and fickle real estate markets. The designer of an ecotourism facility must feel the land and grow into harmony with it as he or she creates this organic architecture. The spirit of the architecture must grow naturally from the earth and dwell lightly on the landscape (Good, 1990). For example, the designer needs to observe the behavior of animals peculiar to the specific property so that placement of the buildings does not interrupt behavioral patterns and habitat. The designer and the developer must spend time together on the site assembling an encyclopedia of understanding about the place and a realization of the harmonies into which the development must fit. The book *Design With Nature* (McHarg, 1992) emphasizes that designers do have choices and it is up to them to make responsible choices for the benefit of nature.

One cannot predict, without this process, the actual forms which may be generated by an organic approach to design. They are an outgrowth of the uniqueness of the site, the development program, and the imagination of the designer. It is safe to say, however, that the uniqueness of a particular site may inspire changes in the development concept that ultimately will enhance the success of the ecotourism facility. The resulting site-specific facility design will support the tourists' experiences and heighten the awareness that a visit is something out of the ordinary, a precious opportunity to learn to appreciate and experience the world.

WORKING WITH LOCAL RESOURCES: A GRASS ROOTS APPROACH TO BUILDING

Ideally, an ecotourism facility is created in part from a dialogue between the local community and the individual developer. If the developer/owner comes from outside the area of development, it is essential to enlist local residents in the planning process as well as in staffing the completed facility. Local involvement makes sense from the developer's perspective for three reasons: local cultural and ecologic knowledge can contribute to the design, it is important to provide local involvement and benefits to ensure long-term support for ecotourism in the area, and such involvement can reduce negative cultural impact.

It is also important to work within the existing community/culture structure as much as possible, recognizing the values of the local people as well as the availability and type of human resources in the area. To work successfully with the community, the developer must invest the time to know where the long-standing family feuds might exist, for example, or which lifestyle habits which might affect the performance of the local work force, or any of a number of other unknown factors affecting the development from a human perspective. Additionally, when an outside labor force must be brought in, it is important to plan for the impact by providing temporary housing for workers and families as a part of the planning process with the local community.

In some remote areas the impact of outside monies may have an adverse affect on the traditional lives of construction workers or operational staff. Inasmuch as it is possible, one needs to anticipate the intrusion of the facility on the local culture. Belizean Tourism Minister Glenn Godfrey noted at the First World Congress on Tourism and the Environment that ecotourism should "allow people to be more, not necessarily have more."

Tourism is a very sensitive industry, subject to the perceptions of the tourist. Security is a large issue for foreign travelers. Facility planning should address the personal security of visitors and their possessions. In addition, local people in areas targeted for tourism development must be given an understanding of the importance of preventing petty crime and other threatening impressions. This may require an educational effort that often transcends the ability of the individual developer. Nevertheless, minimizing nuisance crime and negative interpersonal experiences can go far to enhance the long-term attractiveness of the area.

For the foreign ecotourist, a visit to an ecotourism facility represents a cross-cultural experience. The facility design should recognize the value of providing a supportive setting for this experience while not going too far in trying to provide creature comforts that are in contrast with local lifestyles. Designs that underscore the differences in lifestyle and financial resources may cause subtle resentment within the local population.

Any change in an area, such as the construction of an ecotourism facility, will have an impact on a region. It is not the intent of this writer to advocate "cultural taxidermy." Cultures naturally change and evolve. It is necessary, however, that everything possible be done to reduce the shock of sudden change on the local culture.

A CHECKLIST FOR DEVELOPMENT OF ECOTOURISM FACILITIES

The following generalized criteria are suggested as a guideline for more detailed standards related to specific local issues and the ecological characteristics of a given site. With some exceptions, the criteria and the principles they embody may also be applied to other types of development. They are intended as a general guide only and should not be considered a complete list of criteria or as a substitute for professional services.

SITE PLANNING ISSUES

- Site buildings and structures to avoid cutting significant trees and to minimize disruption of other natural features.

- Use naturally-felled trees whenever possible (such as trees felled by windthrow or other natural causes).

- Trail systems should respect travel patterns and habitats of wildlife.

- Erosion control should be considered in all building/trail placement.

- Divert water off trails and roads before it gains sufficient flow and velocity to create significant erosion problems.

- Shorelines and beachfronts should not be intensively cleared of vegetation.

- Minimize trail crossing points at rivers and streams.

- Maintain vegetation areas adjacent to lakes, ponds, perennial streams, and intermittent streams as filter strips to minimize runoff of sediment and debris.

- Buildings should be spaced to allow for wildlife travel patterns and forest growth.

- Use of automobiles and other vehicles should be strictly limited.

- Provide trailhead signs to enhance appreciation of natural environment and to clearly establish rules of conduct. Provide additional rules posted in guest units.

- Discretely label plant/tree types around the immediate lodging facilities to acquaint visitors with species they may encounter in the surrounding preserved/protected areas.

- Utilize low impact site development techniques, such as boardwalks, instead of paved or unpaved trails wherever possible. (See Figure 5-2.)

- Pastures and corrals for horses and other grazing stock should be located so as not to pollute water sources or watersheds.

- Review any potential sources of sound or smell associated with the development that may be disruptive to the environment or offensive to the visitor.

- Design should reflect seasonal variations such as rainy seasons and solar angles.

- Site lighting should be limited and controlled to avoid disruption of wildlife diurnal cycles.

Special care should be taken in planning of trails through untouched areas. It is prudent to hire a naturalist to help place the trail system to minimize disruption of wildlife and plant biosystems. Special attention should be granted to creatures that rely on trees as aerial pathways or habitat. Careful consideration should be taken in the placement of access roads into a site. Vehicular travel within protected areas should be limited if not avoided completely. A civil engineer should also be involved in the design of trails where erosion control may be an issue. Opportunities for handicapped individuals should be provided wherever possible.

Building Design Issues

- Design of buildings should utilize local construction techniques, materials, and cultural images wherever that approach is environmentally sound.

- Provide building forms and images in harmony with the natural environment. Design buildings on long-term environmental standards and not necessarily on short-term material standards.

- Maintenance of ecosystem should take priority over view or dramatic design statements.

- Provide facilities to accommodate messy activities. Placement of boot scrapers, outdoor showers, etc., become a necessity for successful operation in some areas.

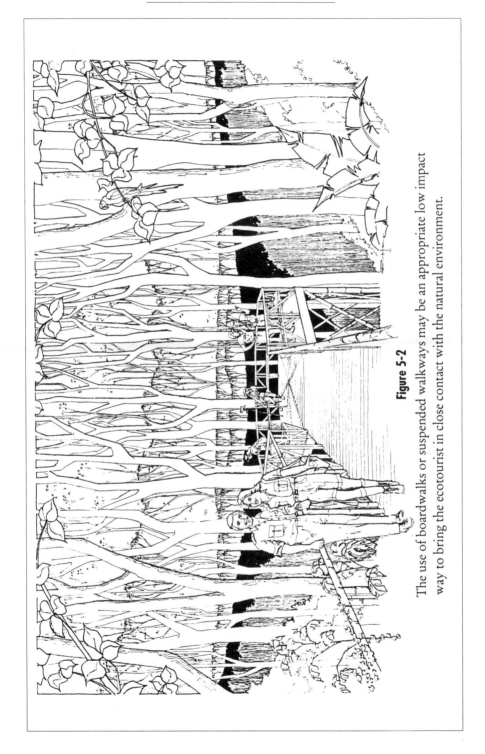

Figure 5-2

The use of boardwalks or suspended walkways may be an appropriate low impact way to bring the ecotourist in close contact with the natural environment.

- Consider use of canopies to cover high use trails between structures to minimize erosion and to provide shelter during the rainy season.

- Provide an architecture consistent with environmental philosophies and/or scientific purposes. Avoid contradictions!

- Provide adequate storage for travel gear, such as backpacks, boots, and other camping equipment.

- Use low tech design solutions wherever possible.

- Prominently post an environmental code of conduct for visitors and staff.

- Provide ecotourists with on-site reference materials for environmental studies.

- Interior furnishing and equipment should represent local resources except where special purpose furnishings or equipment are not readily available from local sources.

- Facilities should take advantage of local materials, local craftsmen, and artists wherever possible.

- Use of energy intensive products or hazardous materials should be avoided.

- Building practices should respect local cultural standards and morals. Involvement of local inhabitants should be encouraged to provide input for the designer as well as a sense of ownership and acceptance by local residents. (See Figure 5-3.)

- Hand excavate footings wherever possible.

- Special design consideration should be given to insect, reptile, and rodent control. The sensitive approach to design should minimize opportunities for intrusion rather than the killing of pests.

- Facilities for handicapped individuals should be provided where practical. It is noted, however, than the rugged nature of most ecotourism or scientific site precludes access for some disabled individuals. Educational facilities should make equal access for the handicapped a strong priority.

- Plan for future growth of the facility to minimize future demolition and waste.

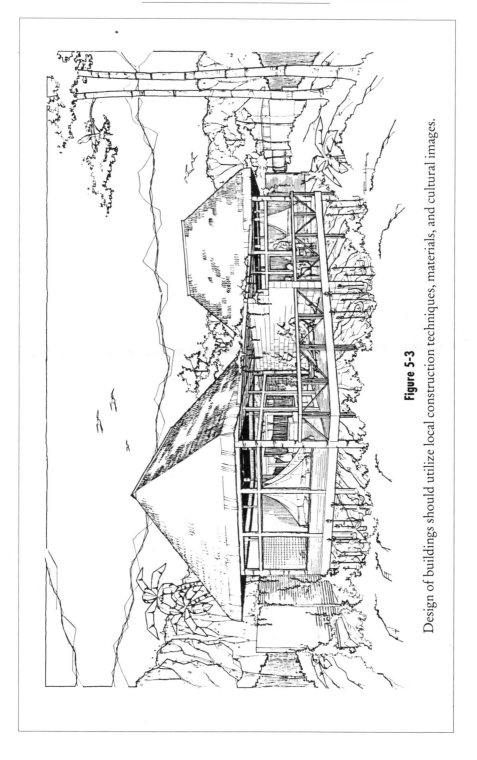

Figure 5-3

Design of buildings should utilize local construction techniques, materials, and cultural images.

- Construction specifications should reflect environmental concerns regarding use of wood products and other building materials. Refer to "First Cut: A Primer on Tropical Wood Use and Conservation," prepared by the Rainforest Alliance.

- Seismic design considerations should also be taken into account.

ENERGY RESOURCE AND UTILITY INFRASTRUCTURE ISSUES

- Landscape elements should be placed to enhance natural ventilation of facilities and avoid unnecessary consumption of energy.

- Consider use of passive or active solar or wind energy sources wherever practical.

- Water lines should be located to minimize disruption of earth, adjacent to trails wherever possible.

- Hydroelectric power generation techniques should be utilized with a minimal disruption to the environment.

- Limit use of air conditioning to areas where humidity and temperature control is necessary, such as computer rooms in research facilities. Design approach should utilize natural ventilation techniques to provide for human comfort wherever possible.

WASTE MANAGEMENT ISSUES

- Provide ecologically sound restroom and trash disposal facilities at trail heads for guests and nonguest use.

- Pastures and corrals for horses and other grazing stock should be located so as not to pollute water sources or watersheds.

- Provide for environmentally sound methods of trash removal.

- Provide trash storage secure from animals and insects.

- Provide facilities for recycling.

- Utilize appropriate technologies for the treatment of organic wastes such as composting, septic tanks, or biogas tanks.

- Look at methods to recycle wastewater for nonpotable uses and to treat tainted waters before their return to the natural environment.

EVALUATING ECOTOURISM FACILITIES:
THE GREEN REPORT CARD

Though establishment of environmental codes of ethics is important for the sensitive development of facilities on the edge of nature, one should not be slavish to such criteria. An absolute approach tends to polarize development from environmental concerns. A more effective solution may be to establish a performance rating system that gives tourist developments a scorecard to inform travel agents and visitors of a particular development's sensitivity to the environment. The pressure of the market-place will then foster a more responsible approach to tourist development.

In creating a "green report card" for evaluating ecotourism facilities, this writer's intent is not to sit in judgment of what is or is not appropriate for ecotourism operators. The intent is to heighten the sensitivity of the operator and visitor alike. The following criteria are primarily directed toward physical facilities and how to evaluate success from a design-oriented viewpoint.

- Is the scale of the development appropriate for the local community and the capacity of the environment to support the facility?

- Were members of the local community actively involved in planning and construction of the facility?

- Are members of the local community involved in the day-to-day operations of the facility?

- Is the facility to be a phased development and if so are the subsequent phases provided for in a manner that allows for minimal disruption to the environment and the existing facility?

- Are roads and trails placed to minimize intrusion on the environment?

- Does the facility design utilize traditional cultural building forms and materials found in the immediate area?

- Does the design of the facility encourage the visitor to look at the natural environment in a new way?

- Are there any contradictions to the ecotourism mission of conservation apparent in the facility?

- Does the facility include a sense of fantasy or any special features that underscore the unique characteristics of the site and surrounding region?

- Are provisions, such as a library, laboratory, or other experimental settings, made to provide visitors with educational opportunities?

- Is the energy source(s) environmentally sound and sustainable?

- Are building materials free of toxic or nonbiodegradable agents?

- Are appropriate technologies employed for the treatment of organic wastes and other wastes? Is recycling practiced?

- Are the building structures and paved areas properly sited to prevent erosion?

- Are the furnishings and other lodging accommodations consistent with the architectural theme and environmental parameters?

- Is accommodation made for older guests and physically disabled individuals?

THE FUTURE FOR ECOTOURISM FACILITIES

From the Ndoki River in the African rain forest to the Trobriand Islands of Papua New Guinea, the last bastions of nature are clearly losing ground against the advance of human development. Conservation of these last fragile pieces of Eden involve a complex set of issues. The advent of ecotourism may be part of the solution, but it should be recognized as only part of a larger environmental and economic picture. It is the obligation of ecotourism facility developers to tread lightly as they design and construct facilities. It is their opportunity to demonstrate their true concerns for the environment and to set an example for their tourist guests.

As one looks at the growth in ecotourism in the last few years it is apparent that there must be limits to this growth. If ecotourism is to live up to its potential for contributing to environmental quality, it must necessarily remain a small niche in the huge global tourism industry. It must remain a grass roots effort firmly based in local economies. It cannot become purely a vehicle for profit. It must be a source of local pride and involvement.

The ecotourism facility itself will remain the visual evidence of sensible sustainable development. The facility is literally the footprint of our concern and understanding. Each facility will be as unique as its environment. Indeed it should be an imaginative extension of the natural world and provide a participatory window for the visitor to nature's creations.

In some countries the development around protected areas is literally choking the natural amenity that has brought development in the first place. In the United States this is all too apparent at some of the most popular national parks. This experience is being repeated in developing countries. Costa Rica's Manuel Antonio National Park is a case in point where the development of hotel and other tourist facilities around the park have changed animal behavior and in some cases eliminated species completely.

If ecotourism development is to be successful, developers and local government must look beyond the singular facility no matter how well-designed or intended it may be. The appropriateness of the facility must be judged in the context of an overall plan for the area. This overall plan should be a product of the interests of both private citizens and the government that represents them. It must also contain the input of the scientific community whose special expertise can give focus to the more sensitive environmental issues and long-term implications of development. It is essential that the sensitivity of the region to accept man's intrusion be established as an overall guideline for development (Leccese, 1992). Zoning of areas for limited use around parks, river corridors, and other environmentally sensitive areas will provide a sensible approach to development. Strict limits on facility development may also be necessary to prevent the wild real estate speculation and overbuilding that can occur when no such limits exist.

With changing demographics in developed countries, tourists will tend to be older in the coming decades. Wherever possible, accommodations should be made in the ecotourism niche to provide a comfortable experience for the older tourist as well as the physically disabled individual.

The architecture of ecotourism should also be viewed as an educational vehicle to enhance the awareness and sensitivity of the ecotourist, scientist, and student. Surveys of tourists indicate that education is one of the most important components of the ecotourist experience, yet it is one of the components that has not been consistently provided. For this reason, the emphasis on nature-based design should be for education as well as to provide creature comforts in an environment often considered hostile to humans. The creation of this kind of participatory educational environment will heighten the experience of the visitor and help to establish an attitude of appreciation for the natural world.

Whenever possible, owners and developers of nature-based facilities should consider the potential uses of a facility beyond the primary intent. Providing multipurpose spaces, for example, can open up a variety of programmatic opportunities for ecotourism operators and educational facilities. Experimental small-scale agricultural efforts can illustrate methods of cultivation in harmony with the environment.

CONCLUSION

If one views the environment as a vast resource library then the ecotourism facility can be viewed as a unique laboratory setting for the ecotourist seeking to gain knowledge. Properly designed, the ecotourism facility can become the window for human awakening to the world.

The 1992 Earth Summit in Rio de Janeiro, Brazil, underscored global awareness that the world is interconnected in its quest for survival. The tourism industry, through the sensitive design of ecotourism facilities, can make a positive contribution to conservation and cross-cultural exchange. Providing the ecotourist with a stimulating experience and comfortable accommodations that have a low ecological impact can be an achievable goal for the ecotourism operator. The beneficiaries go beyond the ecotourist and the ecotourism facility operator. The winners are the local population and our world as a whole. The courage and imagination of the ecotourism facility developer can become the cornerstone of a new awareness. The next generation of ecotourism facilities will be the new window to our natural world.

REFERENCES

Castner, J. L. 1990. *Rainforest: A Guide to Research and Tourist Facilities.* Gainesville, Fla.: Feline Press.

Good, A. 1990. *Parks and Recreation Structures* (reprint of 1938 edition). Boulder, Colo.: Graybooks.

Leccese, M. 1992. "Can Sight-seeing Save the Planet?" *Landscape Architecture,* August, vol. 82, no. 8, pp. 53–56.

McHarg, I. 1992. *Design With Nature* (reprint, originally published in 1969). New York: John Wiley & Sons.

National Park Service. 1992. *Sustainable Design: A Collaborative National Park Service Initiative.* Denver, Colo.: U.S. Government Printing Office.

Wright, F. L. 1954. *The Natural House.* New York: Horizon Press.

ACKNOWLEDGMENTS

A word of thanks to John and Karen Lewis, operators of the Lapa Rios Resort, on the Osa Peninsula in Costa Rica. As our client, it was their dream that initially inspired our pursuits in ecotourism design. Thanks also go to Gail, my wife and business partner, who encourages me to chase far-flung opportunities in ecotourism design.

Basic Steps Toward Encouraging Local Participation In Nature Tourism Projects

Katrina Brandon

Proponents claim that ecotourism "is a mode of ecodevelopment which repre-sents a practical and effective means of attaining social and economic improvement for all countries…" (Ceballos-Lascuráin, 1991). However, even its proponents agree that such claims are more often rhetoric than practice. In many cases, ecotourism has led to numerous problems rather than provide the substantial benefits that may have been intended. Some of the most significant identifiable problems have been ecological damage and environmental degration, negative impact on local culture, and creation of local economic hardships (Ceballos-Lascuráin, 1991; Boo, 1991; West and Brechin, 1991).

Although these problems can be traced to many sources, there are several themes that emerge in the literature which describe why ecotourism has not led to ecodevelopment. The first is an absence of political will and commitment of governments to "mobilize the resources—human, financial, cultural, and moral—to ensure the integration of ecological principles with economic development" (Bunting et al., 1991). Another is the fact that tourism is often promoted by large-scale interests from outside the area. The result is that tourism is not structured to meet local needs and benefits often flow outside the area (West and Brechin, 1991; Wells and Brandon, 1992). Finally, there is the lack of integration of local needs and preferences into the planning process.

In recent years there has been an emphasis on planning and designing ecotourism projects, rather than simply letting ecotourism activities happen based on market forces. There is widespread agreement that "careful planning is necessary to avoid some of the negative side effects of tourism" (Ceballos-Lascuráin, 1991). This trend represents a substantial shift from promotion of a loose collection of activities to planned and organized projects that try to manage and control how ecotourism develops in a given area.

The emphasis of many of these projects has been to promote nature tourism activities that will provide "funds for protected area management and generate income gains for local communities" (Wells and Brandon, 1992). At the core of these projects is the desire to maximize positive local socioeconomic and environmental impact and minimize adverse impact. The 1980 World Conservation Strategy emphasized the importance of linking protected area management with the economic activities of local communities (IUCN, 1980). The need to include local people in park planning and management was adopted enthusiastically by conservationists and protected area managers at the 1982 World Congress on National Parks (McNeely and Miller, 1984). This Congress called for increased support for communities adjacent to parks, through measures such as education, revenue sharing, participation in decision making, compatible development schemes near protected areas, and, where compatible with the protected area's objectives, access to resources. This position was recently reiterated at the 1992 World Parks Congress in Venezuela.

A recent analysis of twenty-three projects attempting to link conservation and development found that many of the projects had initiated nature tourism activities, but few of the benefits went to local people or served to enhance protection of adjacent wildlands (Wells and Brandon, 1992). West and Brechin, in a review of over twenty-five cases, conclude that "there are only certain conditions . . . and planning actions under which the positive economic development benefits will flow to local people" and which can "minimize negative economic, social, and cultural impacts on resident people" (1991). Similarly, another review of ecotourism cases concludes that "a socially responsible and environmentally viable tourism cannot be fostered without a dialogue constructed and controlled along indigenous needs and in indigenous terms" (Johnson, 1990). Johnson (1990), West and Brechin (1991), and Wells and Brandon (1992) together contain descriptions of over fifty programs. Throughout this chapter terms such as "few" or "many" are based on the combined findings of these cases.

This chapter is concerned with ecotourism activities for which providing benefits to local communities is a major objective. The focus deals specifically with *projects* that are designed to provide both conservation and development benefits to communities through nature tourism. Emphasized here are some of the basic issues in working with local communities to ensure that ecotourism development is consistent with local social, ecological, and economic objectives. This chapter focuses on the need for extensive local participation in the ecotourism planning process and identifies ways to do this.

It is evident that there are many cases where a "project" focus may not be appropriate or where providing communities with economic benefits may not be the primary goal. For example, a tour operator may want to work with a local community on changing or improving one aspect of a new or existing tour route. Local entrepreneurs may decide to set up viewing areas, food and craft sales, or lodges. Park officials may want to improve visitor education and lessen the impact of visitors on the environment. All of these are appropriate activities within their own right. However, they represent discrete initiatives rather than the more comprehensive activities targeting local people described herein. Ten specific issues critical to eliciting community-based participation in nature tourism are identified and described on the pages that follow:

- local participation's role

- empowerment as an objective

- participation in the project cycle

- creating stakeholders

- linking benefits to conservation

- distributing benefits

- involving community leaders

- using change agents

- understanding site-specific conditions

- monitoring and evaluating progress

This chapter does not describe the concrete procedures to undertake for each of these steps; there is a vast resource of literature which exists on each of these areas in the rural development context. Finally, it is beyond the scope of this chapter to deal with the external impact that may affect projects and the need to mobilize the political support often vital to successful project implementation.

EXAMPLES OF NATURE TOURISM PROJECTS

Hundreds of nature tourism destinations exist worldwide, but examples of communities which have successfully pursued the dual goals of community development and environmental protection are sparse. Ecotourism is often promoted as a vehicle to link these dual goals. In recent years, many projects have been developed that use nature tourism to link conservation with development. The key objective of these projects is to promote socioeconomic development and provide local people with income sources that do not threaten the natural resource base. These projects are known as integrated conservation development projects or ICDPs (Wells and Brandon, 1992).

Descriptions of two ICDPs, the Annapurna Conservation Area in Nepal and the Monarch Butterfly Overwintering Reserves in Mexico, provide some idea of the challenges in implementing such initiatives. The Annapurna case reflects one of the better examples of careful attention to project design and implementation; the Monarch case demonstrates the difficulties that may be encountered in trying to link ecotourism to local development. More extensive descriptions of each can be found in Wells and Brandon (1992).

One of the most spectacular natural displays in Mexico is the annual migration of billions of monarch butterflies to small reserves in central Mexico. Nearly 100,000 tourists visited one of these reserves in 1989. A lack of economic opportunities in the area, declining agricultural productivity, and increasing poverty have lead to logging, agricultural expansion, and cattle grazing in the core portions of the reserve. A small-scale project initiated by a Mexican nongovernmental organization has attempted to organize visits to the area and has provided an interpretive and visitor center, undertaken revenue sharing (with a portion of gate fees going to the local community), planted trees and maintained trails, and established a community store and booths for food sales. The nongovernmental organization has also worked with the Mexican government to develop an integrated development plan for the region, although the government never adopted the plan.

The site is ideal for nature tourism: it has a highly visible species found nowhere else, high visitation and visibility, and the potential for nature tourism to generate substantial local benefits. Unfortunately, the project has been little involved with the community and has not provided sufficient incentives to stop the destruction of the reserve.

In contrast to the Mexican case, the Annapurna Conservation Area in Nepal covers a large and geographically impressive site. Over 30,000 trekkers visit the region to hike in the Himalayas and enjoy the cultural diversity of the area. The high number of tourists led to the establishment of many lodges and tea houses, which provide benefits to many community members. Tourism has become important to the local economy, but it has also led to serious environmental problems. Forests have been cleared to provide cooking fuel and heat for visitors. Expanding agriculture, water pollution, poor sanitation and litter on trekking routes have all accelerated, compounded by a rapid growth in the resident population.

The Annapurna Conservation Area Project (ACAP) was designed to minimize the negative impact from tourism and promote conservation and the socioeconomic development of the region. Revenue sharing is used for local development, management has been decentralized to local levels, and training has been provided to individuals and local organizations. Local participation included establishing a lodge management committee and reviving a traditional forest management committee that was responsible for enforcing regulations, fining poachers, and controlling timber cutting. As a result, deforestation rates have been substantially reduced, trails are being maintained, and the local populations are increasingly assuming control over the resources.

Both of these projects were designed to use nature tourism as a vehicle to achieve conservation and development objectives. Both were promoted by nongovernmental organizations, although they involved the cooperation and support of the private sector, local people, and numerous government agencies. Yet one significant difference between the two projects was that local people were involved from the beginning in the ACAP project. In contrast, local people were involved in the Monarch project only after the nongovernmental organization and government identified the problems and the activities that were to be the solutions.

LOCAL PARTICIPATION'S ROLE

Nature tourism projects are increasingly seen as providing an incentive for people to manage the wildlands and wildlife in a sustainable way, since the economic benefits distributed to communities depend on this wise management. Many nature tourism projects assume that nature tourism can be a powerful force for conservation by providing benefits to local people. But as will be described later, meeting such conservation objectives requires careful project design so that benefits are appropriately targeted and, in fact, act as an incentive.

Tourism is often the kind of development that can rapidly change the social and economic situation in communities with both positive and negative impact. In both developed and developing countries, communities often feel powerless to influence these patterns of development. Community-managed tourism projects attempt to let communities decide what type of growth they would like to see and then help them implement their plans.

Why must such projects involve local people? There is little likelihood that destructive resource use practices can be stopped without changes in the social and economic situation facing communities. Such changes can best come about if communities can exercise control over their growth and development. In the tourism context, lack of involvement means that tourism is much more likely to have a negative social and economic impact. There is ample evidence that projects which focus on generating economic benefits without effectively encouraging local participation in the identification, design, implementation, or evaluation of development activities are less likely to provide widespread community benefits (Cernea, 1991).

There are some trade-offs apparent when involving local people in ecotourism planning. Initiating local participation activities requires a great deal of time, energy, and keen organizational ability. For many projects, the amount of groundwork required to elicit participation may seem too large and the time may pass slowly. Private sector interests may want quick action and need fast answers to remain competitive. There is also a risk that the needs and desires of local people may differ from one community to the next or may differ sharply in one community. These trade-offs need to be addressed and incorporated into project designs if the real objective of ecodevelopment is to be realized.

Empowerment as an Objective

Local participation has been described as "giving people more opportunities to participate effectively in development activities. It means empowering people to mobilize their own capacities, be social actors rather than passive subjects, manage the resources, make decisions, and control the activities that affect their lives" (Cernea, 1991). *Participatory approaches* involve people in the process of their own development. Local or community participation viewed as a *process* includes, but goes well beyond, simply sharing in social and economic benefits. The participatory process helps people have more substantial control over their own lives. This participatory perspective differs from the *beneficiary approach*, in which people receive benefits but are not empowered. For example, a nature tourism project might create substantial employment for local people in a range of jobs, from guides and guards to food and craft sales. These jobs would be providing an important local benefit, but local people would not necessarily be participating in decision making.

Consultation is another way in which local people can be involved, although there is often a confusion between communication to local people instead of communication with local people (Wells and Brandon, 1992). Consulting with people and getting their opinions is often mistakenly called participation. It is true that getting people's opinions or giving them benefits are both elements of a participatory approach, but neither of these activities empowers people. In a participatory approach, local people are consulted and they have a voice in making decisions.

Unfortunately, most nature tourism projects emphasize a beneficiary approach and decisions about projects, employment, and the overall type of development to be promoted are often made far from the site. Groups involved in planning and implementing nature tourism projects often say they have a strong commitment to working with local people, yet few projects can be identified which are truly participatory or which have initiated the processes to help communities manage their growth and resources more wisely (Wells and Brandon, 1992; West and Brechin, 1991).

In the Monarch butterfly project, people were viewed as beneficiaries and had no involvement in project design. Though some local residents received the "benefits" of increased employment opportunities, they didn't feel any ownership in the project. Even worse, there was considerable sentiment that the high levels of tourism in the community, and the very existence of the butterfly reserve, had led to many negative impacts. In contrast, the Nepal project was designed to help local people learn to manage the area and its resources. Local people were involved from the beginning, identifying what they saw as the problems all the way through to working toward the solutions. Ecotourism planners need to view local people as their counterparts and use both the planning process and ecotourism activities as tools that empower local people to exercise greater control over their lives.

LOCAL PARTICIPATION IN THE PROJECT CYCLE

There is no point too early in the project cycle to begin some process of local participation. The earliest steps involve information gathering: "empowerment starts with access to information" (Johnson, 1990). Reliable information about the community and local preferences is the basis for developing sound ecotourism plans. Gathering information is essential whether the idea from the project came from the community itself or from an outside group. During this phase it is possible to identify: local leaders; what local organizations exist; what the community sees as key priorities; and what ideas, expectations, and concerns people have about ecotourism. Preliminary information can be helpful in starting a more inclusive process of information gathering and sharing.

There are at least five areas where local people can help to bring about nature tourism activities: information gathering, consultation, decision making, initiating action, and evaluation. The process of information gathering and sharing naturally leads into a design phase. For the ACAP project in Nepal, the information gathering and sharing phase was crucial. During the information gathering phase it became clear that there would be massive local opposition to the declaration of a national park in the area. This opposition was the result of concerns and problems caused by resettlement in the process of creating other national parks. The project developed the idea of creating a new protected area classification that would designate a multiuse area, and legislation was passed by the government to establish the Annapurna Conservation Area. Such early information gathering and dialogue can be vital to the success of projects.

Information can be gathered both from the community and by the communuity (excellent discussions on how to do this can be found in Mascarenhas et al., 1991). The knowledge and opinions collected during the information gathering phase need to be presented and discussed with the community, along with other relevant information, such as results from marketing surveys or government plans for the area. Once this information has been disseminated, a process to involve representatives from different groups (consultation) can begin. Discussing this plan within a broader community forum will help strengthen it and lead to implementation as decisions are made and plans begin to take shape. Training may also be an important component of this phase. Local organizations may need strengthening and local people may need some training in skill areas, in order to both run more efficient organizations and to manage or operate tourism ventures or subsidiary services.

CREATING STAKEHOLDERS

One of the functions of local participation is that people have a sense of ownership in projects. In addition to direct participation, there are also a variety of ways that people can become stakeholders in nature tourism activities. One strategy is to promote participation at two levels: individually and as part of an organization. For example, ACAP requires people to contribute cash or labor to community projects, such as reforestation and trail maintenance activities. Yet it also encourages participation on an individual basis. Lodge owners are required to invest in the upgrading of their facilities. In return, the project has promoted individual entrepreneurship by providing lodge owners with training and technical assistance. The project has also worked with groups of lodge owners to develop standards for lodging and meals. As a result of the individual investments in training and in upgrading their enterprises, lodge owners have a stake in the long-term quality of the area.

In the Monarch butterfly project, the benefits flowing from tourism are based on the individual capacity of certain people as entrepreneurs, such as men serving as guides and women selling food. Yet this kind of individual activity does not require a long-term investment, and as a result, few people are "stakeholders" in the outcome of tourism activities. For example, instead of investing in the project through their labor or savings, local people were given food (in effect paid) in return for planting trees. Not surprisingly, few of the trees were maintained once planted since the trees were not seen as "theirs." And local people had little involvement in planning or operating the community store. Similarly, the lack of decision making involvement and control over community receipts from entry fees has led toward apathy over the revenue collected. It is seen as a windfall, not as something which local people control.

Successful tourism creates stakeholders on many levels, involving both individuals and communities through contributions of labor, cash, or other resources. They emphasize local investment and control in addition to local decision making.

LINKING BENEFITS TO CONSERVATION

One justification for many ecotourism projects is that ecotourism can promote conservation action by demonstrating the importance of natural areas for generating tourist income (Ceballos-Lascuráin, 1991). The view is that rural populations have few alternatives to economic activities that degrade or destroy the resource base. Ecotourism is seen as representing a source of employment and income, which should in turn act as an incentive to halt destructive practices. In this view, ecotourism should provide benefits in such a way that they will act as an incentive either for continuing sound resource management practices or abating destructive practices.

One key element as to whether ecotourism will promote conservation depends on how clearly the benefit people receive is linked to protecting the resource base. The benefits (income) from ecotourism often do not stay in the local areas and few local people are involved in tourism in any significant way. In too many cases, benefits are seasonal or jobs are low-level and limited to few people—what West and Brechin call a "hire the natives" approach (1991). Another common problem is that the linkage between the ecotourism benefits and conservation objectives are indirect (Brandon and Wells, 1992). When benefits are low and/or linkages are weak, it is not surprising then that ecotourism does not lead to any conservation action.

The Annapurna project recognized the need to keep economic benefits in the region, involve local people in tourism, and link conservation and development benefits, through tourism, as much as possible. One of the problems facing ACAP was that tourism was resulting in deforestation, as owners of small lodges cut trees to provide heat and hot water for guests. Apart from the conservation benefits of leaving trees in place, it was clearly in the interest of the lodge owners to halt the deforestation in order to protect the beauty of the area and make sure that tourism was sustained. ACAP organized lodge owners and all agreed to honor a requirement that trekking expeditions had to bring in their own kerosene. Additionally, ACAP has provided expertise for lodge owners to install solar panels and recycle heated cooking water, although lodge owners have paid for such improvements with their own money.

There are ways to strengthen the linkage between benefits and conservation objectives to create positive incentives. The benefit must be considered significant to a large portion of the community if it is to be an incentive. In this context, it would be more effective for a small tourism project to convert many potential poachers into part-time guides, rather than hire one or two people full time. The community must exercise some control over the decision making; linkages are stronger if the community has a stake in both the benefits and conservation objectives. The benefits must be flexible over time so as to maintain the interest of different groups within the community. Finally, there must be a good level of community organization to reinforce the linkage.

The bottom line to many nature tourism projects is how to ensure that the income, employment, and other benefits from nature tourism will help sustain the resource base. This can best be done if the link is direct and obvious; in other words, the relationship between conserving the resource base and the receipt of benefits to the community should be clear.

Examples of Design Questions: Benefits as Incentives

What will ensure the best participation? Which activities are a direct link between project objectives and local benefits? Who won't receive benefits under the activities being planned? What kind of long-term investment will local people make in the activities? Who will control decision making? Are there ways activities can be structured to provide multiple benefits, such as employment for some, training for others, and revenue sharing for the community?

DISTRIBUTING BENEFITS

Once there has been some discussion and resolution about the benefits, it is important to consider who will get the benefits, how they will be distributed, and for how long they will be received. "Power structures, whether based within the indigenous community, the state, or the international tourism market, often determine where tourists visit, what they see and do, and who, among the indigenous population, receives the economic benefits of hosting and servicing the guests" (Johnson, 1990). Strong appraisal and participatory processes can identify whether elites and outsiders are likely to capture the benefits that may be generated.

Nepal's ACAP aims to enhance local incomes and management of the natural resources. The project has sponsored a range of activities to encourage broad-based local involvement and decision making. One of ACAP's early goals was to increase the local benefits from tourism and reduce the negative impact of trekkers. The project has been aware that many of the project benefits have been concentrated on local residents with sufficient income to open lodges and tea shops. Project staff have worked with other groups to encourage tree planting and reduce deforestation. They have begun identifying ways to expand the number of people involved and the variety of activities with which they are involved. The project recognizes that both increasing incomes and managing resources is a long, slow process. But the project is trying to provide a moderate level of benefits to a broad group of people. ACAP started by providing benefits to an influential segment of the population (lodge and tea shop owners) who were already better off and had the money to invest in small enterprises. But the project is now moving beyond that to work with a broader spectrum of people.

In the Mexican case, the community level benefits were not apparent to most of the community. The individual benefits were highly limited and dependent on individual entrepreneurship such as who offered the best food and got the best spot for food sales. Thus, the benefits were narrowly distributed and were limited.

Examples of Design Questions: Benefit Distribution

For example, is it best to have a hotel and restaurant run by the community with some revenue sharing, or is it best for individuals in the community to establish lodges and restaurants individually? Is there the local capacity to run it efficiently? Will some people be stuck in long-term subservient positions? Will competition among individual owners erode group decision making and strong management? Is there the tourist demand to justify multiple investments by many people? Are there crafts which can be sold? What organization is most appropriate, collective or individual? Who can serve as guides? What uses of the resources are destructive, which are sustainable, and who in the community affects these uses? If the benefits are widely distributed, will everyone get so little that it is not worth their involvement? Conversely, if the benefits are narrowly distributed will that act as an incentive for others to participate or will it exclude too many people and lead to resentment and income inequality?

Projects work best when a high level of benefits can be provided to many people and when there is evidence to them that these benefits are sustainable. Not everyone has to benefit directly; revenue which provides obvious support for community development projects may be sufficient. A mixture of individual and community benefits may provide the best way of reaching a variety of people in a short amount of time.

IDENTIFYING COMMUNITY LEADERS

One of the first steps in working with communities is to identify the community leaders. Projects sometimes try to start a process of local participation through town meetings. But such meetings usually don't work well unless there has been a history in which project managers can identify and gain credibility with community leaders. The community leaders will, in turn, provide assistance in getting the community together to attend the meeting.

But identifying and working with community leaders is not always as straightforward as it might seem. Project designers need to be aware that there are many kinds of leaders and many sources of power within communities. The most obvious leaders are those who have a formal leadership role, such as the mayor, a clergy member, or shaman or teacher. It is usually relatively easy to identify the people who have some formal role in a community. Formal leaders may be contrasted with opinion leaders — those who people traditionally turn to if they want advice or help on specific problems or issues—who are the local experts. Usually there are many more opinion leaders than formal leaders. Finally, there are leaders who may be hidden—powerful people who control access to financial or other resources in communities. The quick way to identify local leaders is through discussions with community members—either formally, through surveys and interviews, or informally—in places where people gather or in their homes.

Why is it important to identify these different leaders? The simple answer is that the more leaders involved, the better the planning and execution of most projects. Each of the leaders will bring different types of expertise and experience to project design. For example, some leaders are good at planning projects or getting activities started, others are good at getting people involved. The most important reason for identifying different leaders is that the participation of each of these leaders in a process begins to make the project belong to the community.

Another important reason to identify a variety of different community leaders is that each leader may represent a different constituency. Opposition to projects is moderated if leaders can represent community concerns. Also, outsiders planning a project need to make sure that those who might not be well-represented in a nature-tourism project also have a voice. For example, in many societies, men are the formal leaders. Men often do not consider important activities that could benefit or harm women and children when they design projects. Similarly, leaders from different social, economic, or class groups may not take the positions of others into account. In general, people come up with good designs based on who they are and what they know. Therefore, involving both formal and opinion leaders to get strong representation from many groups is important.

It is important to point out than in many cases leaders may not want to work together or meet with one another. In some communities, there may be significant divisiveness among groups and leaders. Strong leaders and existing power structures may not want a participatory process to be initiated that will challenge the status quo and thus their leadership. Clearly, this is important to know in the design of any project. What it may imply is that different groups and leaders participate in different phases or components of the project.

Examples of Design Questions: Identifying Local Leaders

Formal Leaders: Who are the local teachers, healers, agricultural extension agents? Who is the traditional authority? Who are the political leaders? Opinion Leaders: Who knows the most about the forest? Who do you go to if you are sick? Does anyone get agricultural credit? Who lends money? Has anyone worked in a city and returned here? Who contacts the government for the community? Where do you buy things?

Different leadership strengths are often associated with different types of people. For example, people who are willing to promote change and take risks are often younger, better educated, and have contacts outside of the area. People who give a project credibility are older, respected, with greater social or economic positions. People who actually implement projects tend to be oriented toward the community and middle aged (St. Julien, 1989). It is also useful to bring people into project planning who have leadership skills, but may not be regarded as leaders.

BRINGING ABOUT CHANGE: AGENTS AND INSTITUTIONS

Two principal approaches to organizing and sustaining community participation in projects can be identified. The first is employing change agents—people from outside the targeted area. The second major approach to eliciting local participation is through building institutions involved in nature tourism.

In nature-tourism projects, change agents are the outsiders affiliated with conservation, development, or tour operator groups who are interested in introducing nature tourism in communities. "Outside" can mean outside the community, region, or country. Using change agents is often the fastest way to change local ideas, technologies, and introduce new activities into communities.

In most communities there are a variety of formal or informal organizations that exist to group people along one or more similar interests. Three common types of organizations are often found in communities: local development associations, cooperatives, and interest associations. Local development associations often emphasize either self-help methods or put pressure on governments to provide needed services. These groups can serve as an excellent base for nature-tourism activities, since the groups already have development objectives in mind. Cooperatives collect some common element (such as labor, money, or crops) from people and in turn provide some economic benefit to members. Interest groups are less economically based than local development associations or cooperatives and focus on some common characteristic of members (such as gender, occupation, or ethnicity).

Participation through institutions or organizations is more likely to be effective and sustained than individual participation (Uphoff, 1987). Local institutions can act as a focus of mobilization among local people, a way of involving people directly in nature-tourism projects. Organizations can also serve as a link between local people and external organizations, such as governments, nongovernmental organizations, or tour groups.

Local organizations and institutions will be found in most settings. But these organizations may not have the capacity to carry out planning, budgeting, accounting, and evaluation, which can all be important components in promoting community based nature tourism. Projects may have to provide some guidance and training to these institutions to strengthen them. This process of institution building has been defined by Midgeley (1986) as "the creation of procedures for democratic decision making at the local level and the involvement of local people in these procedures to the extent that they [come to] regard them as the normal way of conducting community affairs."

Building local institutions clearly takes more time than working through change agents. These two approaches can often be combined so that change agents work directly with local institutions, which in turn work with their membership on training, and decision making. Combining the two approaches to affect change is one of the best ways to ensure short- and long-term success.

Examples of Design Questions: Identifying local organizations

Are there any religious groups that hold meetings? Is there a credit society? Are there any recreational groups, such as a group that plays soccer or cricket or a theater group? Are people organized in any way by local economic activities, such as fisherman, farmers, loggers, hunters, rattan gatherers, knitters, poultry or livestock raisers? What about people who collect sap, bark, or plants for medicine? Is there a women's or mother's group? A local development society?

Getting people to participate in a project is much easier if they can participate through an existing organization. A group can help set rules, agendas, and establish or use existing procedures to help plan and implement activities. Working with existing groups can be a quick way to work with people from a large area. Meetings can be held with each group individually in the beginning followed by more broadly based meetings, held with one or two representatives from all of the different groups in a community, as well as with local leaders. These representatives can take back questions or plans to their particular group for more discussion or scrutiny. Perhaps the most important question to address in thinking about change is not who will bring it, but what process will be used.

UNDERSTANDING SITE-SPECIFIC CONDITIONS

There are no models of participation or of nature tourism that will work everywhere. Similarly, there are limits to the practical implementation of local participation in many nature-tourism activities. Many of these limitations will be imposed by conditions in the community; other limitations will be imposed by limited funding or a need to quickly bring in tourists. Local participation takes time. It is costly and slower than rushing in and having decisions made from outside the area.

In many societies the authority structures may inhibit extensive participation in decision making or may make it difficult to elicit the opinions of certain groups. In others, strong local organizations may want to emphasize income and employment generation and have little regard for long-term environmental quality. Or different groups may seem unwilling to meet with one another and it may be difficult to reach any type of consensus on what activity is best. Other projects will have involvement from nongovernmental organizations, the community, the government, and private sector. In most cases, cooperation among all of these groups and with government agencies will be necessary for objectives to be achieved. The scale of the project will influence what levels of local involvement are most appropriate.

For example, the Monarch butterfly project has a primary impact on four or five communities, particularly on El Rosario, the community adjacent to the reserve. It would be appropriate to have an intensive process of local involvement in El Rosario, with input from the other affected communities. A similar situation exists in Annapurna, where some villages receive much higher levels of tourism based on how the Annapurna trail is laid out. Participation can be tailored to the level of tourism appropriate to an area, or can more broadly involve the people in a number of communities who are most likely to be affected.

The answer to what is most appropriate depends on the particular socioeconomic and cultural characteristics, and the resources, of each area. Firm answers on what works best are impossible to provide since they change depending on the context. Planning nature-tourism activities means that projects need to be open and flexible in their planning process and need to keep asking local people about the range of possibilities.

MONITORING AND EVALUATING PROGRESS

Projects often give insufficient attention to monitoring and evaluation. Yet it is relatively easy to make monitoring and evaluation part of an ongoing participatory process. When monitoring and evaluation are part of a process it allows adjustments and changes to be made as the project unfolds. Balancing long- and short-term objectives is essential. A participatory approach to stimulating fundamental change is likely to require substantial periods of time before positive results can be clearly identified. Yet without it, long-term successes are impossible. However, the generation of short-term benefits is also likely to be essential in order to establish the credibility of the project locally and to overcome distrust and skepticism among the target population.

Developing some key objectives and indicators for the activities initiated can allow projects to measure the impact of their social and economic development activities, and conservation objectives, so as to provide useful input for future planning. Data emphasizing the community is as important as data on tourism and visitation. Because tourism's impact (both positive and negative) is so well known, it is not too difficult to set up indicators to determine whether ecotourism is leading to ecodevelopment.

Paul (1987) summarizes much of the literature by suggesting that the objectives of a participatory approach to development projects include increasing project effectiveness, increasing the capacity of beneficiaries to take responsibility for project activities, and facilitating cost sharing through local contributions of land, money, or labor. Others have pointed to the importance of involving stakeholders (i.e., intended beneficiaries) in order to give them a vested interest in, and presumably greater commitment to, the achievement of project goals. It is not easy to measure achievements against these kinds of objectives, particularly over short periods of time while projects are still in process, and before more tangible benefits have become apparent. Projects with a beneficiary orientation generally set their goals in terms of readily measurable indices, such as income levels, numbers employed, crafts sold. Improvements in these indices will be taken as representing project success. Many of these measures are important, but they are not sufficient. Nature tourism projects with a participatory orientation will be interested in achieving similar goals to the beneficiary projects; however, they are oriented more towards establishing a process leading to change which will be sustainable beyond the life of the project.

CONCLUSION

Why involve local people in ecotourism? There are lots of reasons, spanning moral, economic, and environmental objectives. From an environmental and economic perspective, if local people are not involved, it is likely that over time, the resources will be destroyed and the investment will be lost. From a moral perspective, it is preferable that local people manage their own destiny rather than be buffeted by outside forces. "Perhaps one of the most significant responses to the problems of tourism is the emerging participation of indigenous peoples in studying, discussing, and devising strategies to control or capture control over the development decision-making process" (Johnson, 1990).

In fact, there is little experience in community based ecotourism planning and management. Although there are relatively few examples of community managed ecotourism, one positive note is that there are more numerous examples of communities jointly managing all kinds of things, from forests to irrigation systems. Although ecotourism is often promoted by conservation groups, the groups with community based experience often have their roots in community and rural development.

> Those in the international conservation community who are in-
> deed sincere about the true intent of ecodevelopment tourism
> need to operate with a clearer social scientific understanding of the

conditions necessary to achieve these objectives for the rural poor, and a coordinated political will to resist the tendencies in the political economy that can tend to thwart those objectives (West and Brechin, 1991).

This chapter has attempted to lay out what some of the issues are for local communities concerned about ecotourism development. Each of the issues attempts to summarize volumes of information about rural development experience and briefly apply it to ecotourism. Generally, the issues summarized here can be grouped into three categories for planning ecotourism projects: who to involve, why involve them, and how to involve them.

The who-to-involve sections looked at the objectives of participation, looked at the role of participation in ecotourism, and argued for making local empowerment an objective of ecotourism activities. Local participation provides a way to make sure that greater benefits remain in the community and that the linkage between incentives and benefits is strong. Furthermore, it provides communities with the knowledge and power to exercise increased control over resource management and development. The section on participation in the project cycle indicated that there is no time too early to begin a participatory process.

The why-involve-them sections discussed the importance of giving indigenous people some stake in ecotourism to improve the chances that tourism will be responsive to local needs. From both an environmental and development perspective, it makes sense for people and communities to actively manage the activities and resources around them. Strong planning and management are essential to maintain or improve the quality of life of local people and of the wildlands and wildlife that surrounds them. Benefits from ecotourism—improved access to resources, income, or employment—are more likely to result in improved resource management and conservation if linkages are clear and direct. Finally, ecotourism is most likely to act as an incentive for conservation and a catalyst for local development if the benefits are widely distributed.

The final section summarizes some of the how-to elements: how to identify community leaders, how to bring about change, how to identify the site-specific conditions that will be important, and the importance of trying to evaluate if ecotourism is leading to ecodevelopment.

Even after addressing all of these issues adequately, as West and Brechin point out, there is the whole array of political issues which may limit ecotourism's potential to contribute to either conservation or local socioeconomic benefits. The most basic element is to insure that the indigenous voice in the development and management decision making process has real political weight (Johnson, 1990). This chapter has attempted to outline a preliminary set of steps to orient tourism activities toward that objective.

REFERENCES

Boo, E. 1991. "Planning for Ecotourism." *Parks*, vol. 2, no. 3, November, pp. 4–8.

Brandon, K., and M. Wells. 1992. "Planning for People and Parks: Design Dilemmas." *World Development*, vol. 20, no. 4, April, pp. 557–70.

Bunting, B. W., M. N. Sherpa, and M. Wright. 1991. "Annapurna Conservation Area: Nepal's New Approach to Protected Area Management," in P. C. West and S. R. Brechin, eds. *Resident Peoples and National Parks*. Tucson: University of Arizona Press.

Ceballos-Lascuráin, H. 1991. "Tourism, Ecotourism, and Protected Areas." *Parks*, vol. 2, no. 3, November, pp. 31–35.

Cernea, M. 1991. *Putting People First: Sociological Variables in Rural Development*. New York: Oxford University Press, second edition.

International Union for Conservation of Nature and Natural Resources (IUCN). 1980. *World Conservation Strategy: Living Resource Conservation for Sustainable Development*. Gland, Switzerland: IUCN, United Nations Environment Programme, and World Wildlife Fund.

Johnson, B. 1990. "Introduction: Breaking out of the Tourist Trap." *Cultural Survival Quarterly*, vol. 14, no. 1, pp. 2–5.

Mascarenhas, J. et al., eds. 1991. *Participatory Rural Appraisal*, Proceedings of the February 1991 Bangalore Participatory Rural Appraisal Trainers Workshop. Rapid Rural Appraisal Notes Number 13, August 1991. International Institute for Environment and Development London and MYRADA Bangalore. (Available from IIED, 3 Endsleigh Street, London WC1, U.K.)

McNeely, J. A. and K. R. Miller, eds. 1984. *National Parks, Conservation, and Development: The Role of Protected Areas in Sustaining Society*. Washington, DC: Smithsonian Institution Press.

Midgeley, J. 1986. *Community Participation, Social Development and the State*. London: Methuen.

Paul, S. 1987. *Community Participation in Development Projects: The World Bank Experience*. World Bank Discussion Paper 6. Washington, D.C.: The World Bank.

St. Julien, N. 1989. *Local Participation*. Unpublished document for the Wildlands and Human Needs Program, World Wildlife Fund. Washington, D.C.: World Wildlife Fund.

Uphoff, N. 1987. "Approaches to Community Participation in Agriculture and Rural Development," in *Readings in Community Participation*, vol. 2. Washington, D.C.: Economic Development Institute.

Wells, M., and K. Brandon, with L. Hannah. 1992. *People and Parks: Linking Protected Area Management with Local Communities*. Washington, D.C.: The World Bank.

West, P. C., and S. R. Brechin, eds. 1991. *Resident Peoples and National Parks*. Tucson: University of Arizona Press.

Ecotourism and Community Development: A View From Belize

Robert H. Horwich, Dail Murray, Ernesto Saqui, Jonathan Lyon, and Dolores Godfrey

In recent years, conservationists have become increasingly concerned with the impact of tourism on developing countries. Despite the allure of tourism as a low-cost high-profit venture, mass tourism can have far-reaching, negative consequences for native peoples and the environment. It can degrade the environment through overvisitation (de Groot, 1983), lead to local inflation (Yamauchi,1984; Puntenny, 1990), and widen the cultural and economic gap between local people and affluent travelers (Britton, 1980; Perez, 1980; Tambiah, 1991; Boo, 1991; Polit, 1991, Peters, 1991).

Ecotourism is not only the fastest growing branch of the travel industry (Ceballos-Lascuráin, 1991), it has also been hailed as a hopeful new approach to both preserving fragile and threatened wild areas and providing people in the developing world with opportunities for community development. Although many enterprises purporting to be ecotouristic are clearly marketing tools for travel promoters, even conscientious aims can fall short of their goals.

Poorly managed reserves or parks can lead to destruction of these areas (de Groot, 1983) and the setting aside of lands used exclusively for nature travelers can leave local peoples beyond the fence, jeopardizing the livelihoods of the rural poor and provoking their opposition.

Genuine ecotourism must be predicated upon a systems perspective that includes sustainability and the involvement-participation of local, rural people in those areas where the greatest potential for ecotourism development can be found. Ecotourism must be seen as a collaborative effort between local people and concerned, informed visitors to preserve wildlands and their biological and cultural assets through support of local community development. By community development we mean the empowerment of existing local groups to control and manage valuable resources in ways that not only sustain the resources but also meet the social, cultural, and economic needs of the group.

TOURISM IN BELIZE

Belize, with its impressive combination of natural and cultural features, has become a popular travel destination. Between 1980 and 1990, tourist arrivals increased by 55 percent (Boo, 1990b). In 1984, responding to this influx and the potential tourist-dollar revenues, the government of Belize designated tourism as the second priority for strategic growth. The "Integrated Tourism Policy and Strategy Statement" of 1988 set several important goals, including the creation of a friendly climate for development investment (Boo, 1990b). Much of the initial tourism went to the Cayes, but with the recent emphasis on ecotourism a good percentage is getting inland. However, little money is spent in rural villages.

Belize has devised modernization projects to capture tourism industry potential, such as completing its new airport, building several large hotels, renovating the local market in Belize City, and improving public utilities in the two major urban areas, Belize City and Belmopan. Most significantly, environment was formally connected to tourism in the Ministry of Tourism and the Environment, with its mandate of protecting and enhancing the environment through ecotourism (Godfrey, 1990). A stated emphasis is also local control of small tourist operations at every stage, from ownership and management to service positions (Godfrey, 1990).

Due to Belize's success in developing an ecotourism industry, both the government and the private sector consider wildlife and forest conservation important. The industry has attracted foreign income by using natural areas without building major facilities or drastically changing the sites. Under the Belize Audubon Society, park development and conservation have been integrated with local economic development by promoting local trail guides, local crafts industries, and "bed-and-breakfast" tourism. This local development has been most significant in both the Community Baboon Sanctuary, which has been cited as functioning as a transition area of a Biosphere Reserve (Hartup, 1989), and the Cockscomb Basin Wildlife Sanctuary (Boo, 1990b).

THE COMMUNITY BABOON SANCTUARY

The Community Baboon Sanctuary (CBS) was initiated by Dr. Robert Horwich with the cooperation of twelve landowners in Bermudian Landing, a rural village thirty-three miles northwest of Belize City. The CBS has been an experiment in conservation and multiple land-use methods on private land (Alderman, 1990; Horwich, 1988, 1990; Horwich and Lyon, 1988). Because the majority of wildlands are private, and many landowners understand both the freedom and responsibility

ECOTOURISM: A GUIDE FOR PLANNERS AND MANAGERS

of owning land, conservation efforts have been directed toward the subsistence needs and agricultural practices of area farmers and small ranchers (Lyon, 1986).

The CBS was started in 1985 to encourage private landowners to manage their lands for the benefit of the black howler monkey, *Alouatta pigra*. Because the CBS depends on the landowners' complete cooperation, it must meet their needs as well as those of the wildlife. The basic principle is simple. Private landowners are asked to voluntarily pledge to follow a land-use plan created for each farm in order to maintain a good habitat for the black howler monkey. The goal is to maintain a skeletal forest from which howler troops and other wildlife can easily use the regenerating cut forests. Landowners are asked mainly to leave forest strips along riverbanks, between property boundaries around yearly milpa cuts, and as aerial pathways in large cut areas for the monkeys, as well as to leave specific food trees. These management plans also help landowners reduce riverbank erosion and reduce the fallow time for adequate nutritional buildup between slash-and-burn cultivations.

The first step in the creation of the CBS was in circulating a petition that was signed by most of the villagers of Bermudian Landing including the village council members, inviting Horwich and colleagues to investigate a potential sanctuary. Given this informal acceptance, they then mapped the lands of the twelve villagers who owned farms surrounding the village. They drew up management plans and procured voluntary pledges from the landowners. The pledges were easily agreed to because of their voluntary nature and the fact that the farmers had adequate land. Having a local man act as an intermediary was also very important. Horwich then brought the idea of a community sanctuary before a village meeting with the area representative present. The area representative, an elected official for the area, initially spoke out against the idea. Conservation and ecotourism were then new and exotic concepts in Belize and the area representative, with little background or understanding of conservation, was reluctant to endorse the project. However, once the villagers understood the voluntary nature of the pledge they enthusiatically and unanimously accepted the idea and requested that Horwich try to attract tourism to the village. Since the lands were all privately owned, the national government was neutral toward the sanctuary. It was only after the sanctuary was publicized and tourism increased that government officials became interested in it.

With the aid of the World Wildlife Fund of the United States (WWF-US) and Jon Lyon, a botanical ecologist, the sanctuary has expanded to include over a hundred landowners and eight villages, encompassing eighteen square miles (forty-seven square kilometers) of forest along the Belize River, home to more than a thousand black howler monkeys. Lyon brought the project before each of the other villages at a village meeting and received the same unanimous approval. The CBS continues to grow under the financial support of the Zoological Society of Milwaukee County given to the Belize Audubon Society (BAS).

In 1987, under the BAS administration, the first local Belizean sanctuary manager, Fallet Young, was hired and an operational plan was established. As part of the operation manual written by Horwich, Lyon, Young, and Mick Craig, the executive director of BAS, an advisory committee was created to work with the BAS in administering the sanctuary. With the sanctuary under local management and control, the foreigners took on an advisory role, primarily developing programs. Most of the day-to-day decisions were left to the manager who reported to the BAS director.

Since there was no university and little expertise available in Belize, and since the sanctuary manager did not have a high school degree, Horwich and Lyon provided training and tutorial assistance using high school biology texts. Horwich and Lyon also proposed ideas for programs incorporating the manager's suggestions and wrote the guidebook and field sign texts that the manager used as a formal basis with which to integrate his own forest knowledge. Young was also a trainee at an in-country conservation workshop sponsored by World Wildlife Fund. With this on-site training, Young was then able, eventually, to tutor his assistant and other staff members.

The duties of the manager included meeting yearly with landowners, guiding tourists, and coordinating tourist visits with local hosts. Later in that first year an assistant manager was hired by the BAS. Together the manager and assistant manager gave field lectures to student classes, gathered data on plant phenology, cared for the museum, cut and maintained trails, planted a small arboretum and greenhouse, and performed other maintenance chores. The sanctuary manager handled donations and museum sales as well as hired and paid part-time workers and guides. Since the manager arranged for all economic operations, this eventually led to some claims of unfairness, and jealousies developed. With no functioning advisory committee in place, these problems continued. The BAS is currently working to rectify this situation by creating a strong managerial committee of landowners from each village to oversee on-site operations and implement the sanctuary's four main goals: conservation, education, research, and tourism.

CONSERVATION

The sanctuary manager's most important function is to work with each landowner to make sure agricultural practices are consistent with the management plans they pledged to uphold. The increase in the howler monkey population shows that the conservation plan has been effective. Because nine out of ten landowners are living up to their pledges, part of this increase is attributed to improved farm management practices. This initial success has encouraged efforts to protect other native species as well.

A second endangered species, the Central American river turtle (*Dermatemys mawii*) which is assiduously hunted for subsistence and economic exploitation, rapidly disappears whenever exploited (Moll, 1986). Seasonal reproduction information on the species is being used to make management suggestions to local and federal governments for the turtle's protection and sustained use. The sanctuary also plans to reintroduce plants and animals that have disappeared from the area, including game birds such as the ocellated turkey and hardwoods like mahogany.

EDUCATION

The sanctuary's educational program is designed for a wide spectrum of people including local villagers and school children, Belizeans countrywide, and foreign visitors (Horwich and Lyon, in press). The small natural history museum, Belize's first museum, opened in April 1989. A labeled forest trail and an extensive book on the sanctuary's rain forest are also part of the educational program.

Originally the museum was to be a conservation-oriented resource center available to rural people responsible for protecting the forests in which they live. It has since become an important tourist attraction as well. The exhibits illustrate the importance of tropical forests, forest regeneration after slash-and-burn agriculture, water resources, mutualism, and other ecological topics in a conservation context. They include locally gathered natural history, cultural, archaeological, and historical materials.

The book, *A Belizean Rain Forest: The Community Baboon Sanctuary* (Horwich and Lyon, 1990), started out as a small pamphlet given to local villagers on howler monkeys. Evolving through guidebook stages, it became a 420-page text, integrating information on local flora and fauna with general material on the functions and the importance of tropical rain forests. The book is given free to Belizean schools and is sold to tourists, with profits benefiting the sanctuary.

The three-mile trail system provides visitors with information about the forest through numbered signs whose texts are included in *A Belizean Rain Forest*. Sanctuary staff guides supplement the text with prepared lectures as well as first-hand knowledge about the monkeys. Their familiarity with the forest and local wildlife enhances the educational experience for visitors by incorporating formal with informal conservation education messages.

A 1988 Belize television documentary stimulated Belizeans' interest in the sanctuary. Since then, school class visits have dramatically increased with hundreds of students occasionally visiting in a single day. Added staff are working to regulate these visits and to broaden the lecture program to include rural and Belize City schools. Free booklets on specific topics (howler monkeys, rain forests) and the book have been offered to elementary and high school teachers throughout Belize.

RESEARCH

Research provides the basis for sanctuary management and education, and researchers become long-term tourists who contribute economically to their headquarter villages. Projects have included studies of howler ecology and behavior, forest ecology and farming practices, river turtle biology, bird behavior, pesticide and herbicide residues in fish, cultural studies and studies of landowner views of sanctuary conservation, and tourism (Hartup, 1989).

TOURISM AND LOCAL ECONOMICS

Integrating human interests with the conservation of the forests and wildlife is one of the sanctuary's main goals. Since the villagers first proposed the creation of a tourism base, visits by foreign and Belizean tourists have increased from an estimated ten to thirty visitors in 1985 and 1986, to 200 in 1987, 900 in 1988, 5,500 in 1989, and over 6,000 in 1990.

A few rooms can be rented from local families and overnight tourists can also camp when taking meals with local families. A few tourists use local boat and horseback guides. All of these services are arranged through the sanctuary staff.

An $11,000 grant from the Inter-American Foundation has been used for low-interest loans to villagers. The grant proposal was written by BAS staff and Horwich and was submitted by BAS to the InterAmerican Foundation. Loans were made to five villagers based on proposals they submitted to BAS through the sanctuary manager. The repayment was scheduled to be collected through the sanctuary manager. However, with a change in sanctuary staff, payments ceased for a while. BAS has since arranged for the collection of these payments through the sanctuary committee.

HISTORY OF ECOTOURISM IN THE COMMUNITY BABOON SANCTUARY

At first, considering the lack of tourist amenities and resources, the idea of promoting the area as a tourist destination seemed absurd. As news spread and visitors flocked to the sanctuary, the potential for tourist development became apparent. In 1987, fifteen American students who went to Bermudian Landing to study monkeys provided a trial run of villager accommodation to groups of visitors. The students took their meals with a half dozen families in the village and lived in tents on the host families' properties. It was workable and the program was continued for three sessions in the 1987-1988 season.

All the while, tourism was developing informally. Local teenagers were encouraged to serve as guides, entry to the sanctuary was free, and arriving tourists were matched with local families eager to offer bed-and-breakfast services. More visitors arrived every year.

With the influx of U.S. guided tour groups in 1988, the newly appointed staff quickly saw a need for regulating visitor activities. Tour leaders often circumvented local guides and took their groups through the forest trails on their own initiative. The trails are on private property with livestock fences, planted fields, and other assets, so uncontrolled traffic can cause damage to crops and can reduce protected wildlife populations (Lippold, pers. comm.). Unmanaged visitation also prevented direct contact between local sanctuary staff and tourists who wanted to give money for conservation, specifically to the CBS. Visitors were subsequently required to pay $2.50 per person and to be accompanied by sanctuary staff. Additional donations are also accepted and turned over to BAS for deposit in a CBS account. A small amount is retained for purchases or expenses incurred by the sanctuary manager who is accountable to BAS staff. All of these BAS functions are gradually being turned over to the local sanctuary committee.

Since the sanctuary needed a centralized location to welcome visitors, the museum, which also houses the sanctuary's main headquarters, was created partly for that function. The headquarters helped to formalize and consolidate the sanctuary manager's role, office, and administrative duties. The museum thus accommodates a totality of integrated activities. Despite the trepidations of funding agencies that the museum would receive too little use to justify even its low cost of $12,000, it has become a tourist attraction in its own right.

COCKSCOMB BASIN WILDLIFE SANCTUARY

The idea of a village-based, locally-managed conservation has found its way into other BAS-sponsored projects as well. Cockscomb Basin is one such example that is working for the benefit of local villagers, but it began on a rather different course from the CBS project.

The Cockscomb Basin Wildlife Sanctuary was declared a protected area in 1984 after the jaguar ecology study by Dr. Alan Rabinowitz of the New York Zoological Society. In 1986, 3,600 acres of the Forest Reserve was declared a sanctuary for the jaguars and other wildlife as well (Boo, 1990b). With the success of both the park and the general increase in ecotourism in Belize, the sanctuary has been expanded to 102,000 acres, a realistic size for jaguars (Anonymous, 1990).

Prior to the establishment of the park, a small village of Mayan Indians was located at Quam Bank, where the new park headquarters were to be situated. Once the park was established, the Mayans were compelled to vacate the area without any adequate explanation. As development proceeded in setting up of signs and the installation of a foreign caretaker in residence, the displaced Mayans had little understanding of what was occurring and it appeared to them that their legal rights were being violated. Eventually the people were relocated to a new settlement at Maya Center six kilometers from the original location. Although two local men from the village were hired as wardens, there was still resentment by the villagers toward outside visitors who passed through the village and showed no interest in them. Additionally, villagers were now forbidden to hunt or fish in the newly protected area.

A Peace Corps volunteer was assigned through the Belize Audubon Society as an interim manager in 1985, but there were still very limited relations with the villagers. In 1987, Ernesto Saqui, a local Mayan teacher, was appointed director of the sanctuary. With this local appointment, relations between the park and the villagers improved and villagers also began to see potential economic benefits from ecotourism. Seven young villagers were trained to conduct organized tours, but had to compete with foreign guides.

Despite its remote location, along a poorly maintained six-kilometer road, park visitation has grown from twenty-five in 1985, to 376 in 1986, 1,653 in 1987, 1,909 in 1988, 2,073 in 1989, and 2,017 in 1990. Most visitors to the sanctuary are foreigners and students from Belizean schools including the University College of Belize and Belize Teachers College.

Gradually, economic benefits to villagers began to materialize. At first these were as salaries earned by local cooks and other service providers. As visitation increased, village women sold embroidery and other handicrafts at the roadsides. This haphazard approach met with some success, but eventually the park director and the village council came up with a more organized plan. The villagers built a small thatched building as a craft and souvenir center. The Belize Audubon Society, as part of their park administrative duties, organized several workshops on marketing, quality diversity in craftsmanship, accounting, and bookkeeping, to teach the local craftswomen business skills. Profits soared 87 percent in just one year. In three-and-a-half years, fifteen village women have earned $28,000.

The park now has a few cabins with cooking facilities as well as camp grounds for overnight visitors. The trails are extensively developed and well-maintained. A visitor center with exhibits on the jaguar and the other cats and their prey opened in 1992.

There have been some research projects by foreign scientists including studies of the jaguar and other cats, bird population censuses, and vegetation surveys. The director gathered data in preparation for reintroducing howler monkeys to the sanctuary. Since surrounding forests are being rapidly removed to establish citrus groves, howler troops are being moved into the park from the Community Baboon Sanctuary. Three troops were successfully translocated in 1992, and translocations will continue for two more years.

Problems and Potentials of Village-Based Tourism

Several problems have arisen in promoting tourism in the Community Baboon Sanctuary, partly because of inexperience in creating reserves and lack of tourism planning. Because of the isolated location of the sanctuary, more effort was invested in publicizing the area than in providing an infrastructure for visitor overnight accommodations. In retrospect, a small hotel should have been built and operated by a village or sanctuary cooperative. Instead, foreign interests have attempted to capitalize on the area's success by planning to build hotels in the area. This would undermine the community-based foundation for the entire integrated system, and local people will suffer the disenfranchisement experienced elsewhere.

The lack of a broad-based management structure presents another problem. The Community Baboon Sanctuary was organized under the Belize Audubon Society, because it was the only Belizean-managed and controlled conservation organization. At the time, the society had a full-time executive director and staff and was supported by funding from a U.S. conservation group. When finances were prematurely withdrawn and the BAS executive director's position discontinued, the sanctuary staff was left without direct supervision. For two years the sanctuary staff was supervised only by the BAS voluntary board of directors. Since no local committee was in place, an inordinate burden and responsibilty was placed on the sanctuary manager during this time. Before organizing and promoting the reserve, a committee of village landowners should have been formed. A legal cooperative would have involved more community members in the ground-level process of planning and implementation and might have headed off some of the intravillage and intervillage jealousies that arose.

Resources and communication have presented still other obstacles. A radio, replacing the inconvenient community telephone, has allowed direct communication between sanctuary staff and tourists through the Belize Audubon Society office. Villagers have had an opportunity to obtain revolving loans to add bed-and-breakfast facilities to their homes, but few families are able to take advantage of it, because there initially was a failure in creating a suitable loan collecting mechanism. Maintaining a steady rate of overnight tourism has also been difficult. Currently Gail Bruner of Zoo Atlanta is creating a plan to spread tourism to all the communities in the sanctuary.

Although it is difficult to estimate the economic benefits from ecotourism, Hartup's (1989) tourism data lets us make some estimate. Using the approximately 3,000 foreign visitors in 1990, times the collective amount spent locally (excluding donations) by all interviewed tourists, divided by the number of tourists, gives an estimate of U.S. $21,605 spent in the village during 1990. Of this estimate 8.7 percent was spent on transportation, 9.8 on guiding, 20.2 on accommodations, 43.2 on meals, 12.3 on souvenirs, and 5.7 on personal/other. A second estimate based on the percentages of tourists who spent one and over two nights in the village, times 3,000 visitors times an estimate of what they spent on local travel, meals, and accommodations gives a similar estimate of $20,169 spent in 1990. Most of that money goes to between six and ten of the approximately twenty families in the village. However, much of that money probably stays in the community through local purchases and hiring local labor but that is more difficult to estimate.

The successes of the sanctuary project are promising, although some of its contributions are intangible. Most people in the area feel the project has been beneficial and want it continued. Press, radio, and television coverage have swelled regional and national pride. More people arrive every year, paying local families for bed and breakfast, guide services, and other spin-offs from tourism. The proliferation of howler monkeys shows that local cooperation in conservation endeavors works, which offers encouragement for future projects based on private lands and local subsistence patterns. Not all reserves have to be carved from pristine plots of wilderness to be effective.

The Community Baboon Sanctuary has also had at least one fortuitous result that will further stimulate tourism. The opening of the museum with its exhibit on local Creole culture and history marked the beginning of a yearly festival that has refocused community attention on its cultural tradition. As the sanctuary has developed and more and more visitors have begun to arrive, ethnic consciousness has also risen among the Creole villagers. Creole folk singing, story telling, and bushcrafts have seen a renaissance along with traditional uses of tropical forests. These forest uses include boiling chicle sap for chewing gum, carving wood dishes, making fly brushes, tongs, and fish traps, and processing cohune palm cooking oil.

Most important, the sanctuary has awakened a sense of pride and achievement and has stirred a widespread ecoconsciousness with its own momentum. This gradual, intangible education has integrated an awareness of conservation into the villagers' daily lives. Insights gained at Bermudian Landing through trial and error are now being used in planning a new comprehensive, integrated ecotourism-conservation project in Belize.

MANATEE COMMUNITY RESERVE

Landowners, villagers, and foreign visitors have embraced the community conservation concept, and the CBS model is being applied elsewhere in Belize. One American biologist has organized foreign landowners on Ambergris Cay, a large northern island, to protect the nesting beaches of sea turtles. In Monkey River in southern Belize, a local cooperative has been formed to create the Monkey River Nature Preserve as a tourist attraction. Another project in planning, the Manatee Community Reserve, is even more promising because it integrates protected government lands with private lands and is attempting to overcome some of the experimental mistakes made in setting up the CBS, namely, it has created a legal cooperative with a broad local base to oversee the sanctuary and is constructing a hotel to be run by the local cooperative.

The Manatee Community Reserve (MCR) project began with a series of visits to the area by Horwich and Chris Augusta, an American artist who has visited the area for the last ten years. They presented a plan to the villagers at a village meeting and obtained signatures of support from most of the villagers at the meeting, inviting them to proceed with the plan. A preliminary proposal was then submitted to the village council of Gales Point and to the Minister of Tourism and the Environment, who is also the area representative. The area representative then arranged a village meeting in which a number of politicians and government officials gave short presentations to the villagers. Talks were given by the Minister of Tourism and the Environment, the Chief Justice who is from the village, the Chief Forestry Officer, a government archeologist, a successful foreign hotel entrepreneur and Horwich. The talk by Horwich included potential shortcomings to such a project as well as the potential gains.

At the request of, and with financial support from, the Minister, and with help from the Lands and Forestry Offices, Horwich and Lyon (1991) created a proposal for a multiple-use, land-management plan. The proposed Manatee Community Reserve being planned by the authors and other volunteers (Community Conservation Consultants) covers 170,000 acres of public and private land and three large lagoons.

The specific tourism and local development objectives of the MCR are threefold: first to develop a locally supported reserve to insure sustainable use of resources; second to maintain and strengthen the local rural culture (based on farming, fishing, and hunting); and third to give the village a supplementary source of income through tourism, resulting in economic self-sufficiency rather than traditional job creation. Change will occur gradually, in accordance with community wishes, and under community control. Conservation will encompass preservation of the rural lifestyle as well as protection of wildlife and other natural resources. The sanctuary will concentrate on developing tourism around the community lifestyle, giving tourists an authentic experience of village life, something like the exposure to Creole culture at the Community Baboon Sanctuary. Allowing tourists to enjoy an "intercultural experience" should also relieve villagers of pressure to invent a sense of opulence for tourists (Moulin, 1980).

Because the area around the village of Gales Point has to be viewed in its entirety, the multiland use plan includes subsistence and citrus farming as well as ecotourism (Horwich and Lyon, 1991). Using the biosphere philosophy, the plan provides for core areas where human disturbance will be minimal, buffer zones where specific human uses are designated, and transition zones where human activities will be restricted to ensure proper land use. Human use will be limited to low-impact ecotourism in core areas, which were selected for specific endangered species, specific ecosystems and watershed protection. Buffer zones will be used mainly for selective hardwood logging, managed hunting and gathering, or harvesting nonwood forest resources such as chicle. Based on current human use, transition zones were selected as areas for sustainable agriculture and ecotourism. Zoning restrictions will be used to insure sustainability of both enterprises .

The government-sponsored hotel being built will be run by sanctuary staff under guidance from a local cooperative. This infusion of government seed money has already enticed residents to begin building their own tourism facilities. Systematic record keeping and monitoring of tourist traffic is planned to provide essential data for future tourist planning. Simple research questionnaires with regular follow-up can yield much information about the tourists visiting a given site (Boo, 1990a and 1990b; Hartup, 1989).

In developing the Manatee Community Reserve, as with all ecotourism projects, changes required by tourism have to be carefully balanced so as to keep the cultural unity and integrity of the village intact. CBS guides are encouraged to embellish tours with their own local cultural knowledge about plants and animals. A similar approach would be useful for the MCR guides working out of Gales Point.

In order to better display and protect natural areas, adequate preparation is required. To minimize environmental problems, all tourists should be guided into an area or at least provided with a set of trail maps and rules which can be enforced. Trail systems must be maintained for ease of passage and to keep tourists in selected areas. A similar system of boat channels will have to be laid out in the lagoons for motorized boat traffic, specifically to protect manatees and other wildlife. Lagoon boat channels may include marked water lanes and speed limitations within certain areas. To develop and foster success in ecotours, it is beneficial to locate and mark specific areas where tourists will be most likely to view wildlife or other natural features. By establishing such areas and by pointing out locally unique elements that tourists may not see or understand themselves, the success of ecotours increases. For example, at the Community Baboon Sanctuary, tourists are almost certain to see howler monkeys because guides know where and how to find monkeys. At Gales Point, certain areas where manatees and American crocodiles reside would please naturalists. Setting up permanent viewing sites such as an anchored raft or a viewing tower in these situations would further enhance the possibility of viewing wildlife. Often things that villagers and local guides take for granted will thrill foreign visitors.

Finally, with an eye to pleasing tourists, Gales Point villagers should appraise their village. With village consensus, improvements might include alternative toilets to accommodate both village and tourist wastes. Dry wastes could be recycled to enrich the soils for local flower or vegetable gardens. Planning and constructing boat moorings and piers should be under strict local control.

SUGGESTIONS FOR COMMUNITY-BASED ECOTOURISM PLANNING

Ecotourism, though a growing approach to conservation and development, is still in the experimental stage. We thus can learn from the failures as well as the successes of various projects around the world.

Though some areas, such as the Galápagos Islands, are already experiencing the devastation of overvisitation (de Groot, 1983), projects such as those in Nepal and Ladakh are arising to counteract environmental degradation (Passoff, 1991; Puntenney, 1990; Goering, 1990). Some projects simply fail due to lack of local control, such as at Hana, Hawaii (Farrell, 1990). Those that appear to be more successful are those that are locally managed such as the Kuna tribal tourism operations (Howe, 1982; Chapin 1991). The most promising ventures are those that were established initially at the local, village level, utilizing an integrated approach with an emphasis on appropriate infrastructure and local materials, such as the Tourism for Discovery program in Senegal (Saglio, 1979).

With these and other examples of success, combined with our own experience in Belize, we offer some suggestions for future community-based ecotourism planning.

Village level. Any plan that includes use of local resources must be planned and implemented at the village level, even if the project has a wider scope.

Local integration. Genuine ecotourism must integrate local people as equal partners into the design, implementation, and every other aspect of projects that use lands and resources that are part of their subsistence patterns (Boo, 1990b). The local partners must also benefit from and recognize the partnership between conservation and community development.

Broad-based, legal, local empowerment. Local peoples must become educated advocates for conservation, empowered to manage and administer long-term efforts as conscientious stewards of precious wild resources. Projects must be broad-based with wide involvement rather than based on elite village factions or individuals. Legal organizations must be established to run parks or tourism programs. Thus there must be a strong educational component.

Use existing resources. Among the resources to be used are local human skills, labor, and materials which should be made available through local people and the park centers. Tour leaders and planners should use local staff or local guides and encourage purchases of materials from local people.

Appropriate scale. Design and development should be on a scale appropriate to local lifestyles, social structure, cultural world view, subsistence patterns, and community organization. Ecotourism should be only considered a supplementary industry and an emphasis should be placed on maintaining the existing agricultural, fishing, or other rural industries.

Sustainability. Work for long-term sustainability and perpetuity of conservation efforts. Donor agencies and funding organizations must become aware of the need for long-term commitment of resources to assist community development and conservation. In any village oriented conservation project, financial support must be obtained for immediate village run tourism facilities.

Local needs and conservation are primary. Tourist needs must be made secondary to the preservation of natural areas and their resources, including local people. Tourism projects must be designed to attract those ecotravelers who recognize their role as preservationists and who are willing to provide economic incentives for protection of these resources. Such tourists will be willing to forgo the luxury, convenience, and costly amenities of the mass tourist trade to experience the authentic natural and cultural experiences that are becoming rare. Ecotourists should be informed rather than entertained, educated rather than diverted. Tourists and tour groups must be gently controlled according to the needs of the natural resources and the needs and wishes of local people. Tour group leaders in strategic positions have an obligation to educate clients.

Professionals must contribute. Biologists, anthropologists, and other on-site researchers should tailor some of their study to include hands-on work to involve local people in the responsibility and benefits of conservation.

Conservation is a viable development strategy. National governments must be encouraged to set policies for preserving wildlands as viable development strategies and for reforming land tenure systems so that local rural people can own land without a concomitant obligation to clear, graze, or cultivate their parcels in entirety.

Government support. Governments as well as national conservation groups must actively support local people in ecotourism. This includes financial support, legal support and the creation of a bridge between local-level organization and federal government systems.

Conscientious tour operators and investors. Tour operators who offer "ecotourism" destinations must work through the local communities and local tourism structures. Tour leaders must be thoroughly versed in local life and ecology and must incorporate educational components in their work. They should encourage visitors to purchase materials from the sanctuaries and let visitors know how they can support and contribute to conservation of any site they visit. Foreign investors should be encouraged to invest in community-based ecotourism projects as equal partners with local communities or local investors. As an example, a foreign investor who shows an interest in taking on a village as his partner can be introduced to various villages, with the goal of developing a hotel and selling it, eventually, to a village cooperative.

REFERENCES

Alderman, C. L. 1990. "A Study of the Role of Privately Owned Lands Used For Nature Tourism, Education and Conservation." Manuscript for Conservation International, Washington, D.C.

Anonymous, 1990. "CBWS Expanded. Protected Area Now 102,000 Acres." *Belize Audubon Society Newsletter*, vol. 22, no. 3, pp. 1, 5.

Boo, E. 1990a. *Ecotourism: the Potentials and Pitfalls*, vol. 1. Washington, D.C.: World Wildlife Fund.

———. 1990b. *Ecotourism: the Potentials and Pitfalls*, vol. 2. Washington, D.C.: World Wildlife Fund.

———. 1991. "Ecotourism: A Tool for Conservation and Development," in J. A. Kusler, ed. *Ecotourism and Resource Conservation*, vol. 1. Ecotourism and Resource Conservation Project.

Britton, R. 1980. "Shortcomings of Third World Tourism," in I. Vogeler and A. R. de Souza, eds. *Dialectics of Third World Development*. Montclair, N.J.: Allanheld, Osmun and Company.

Ceballos-Lascuráin, H. 1991. "Tourism, Ecotourism, and Protected Areas," in J. A. Kusler, ed. *Ecotourism and Resource Conservation*, vol. 1. Ecotourism and Resource Conservation Project.

Chapin, M. 1990. "The Silent Jungle: Ecotourism Among the Kuna Indians of Panama." *Cultural Survival Quarterly*, vol. 14, no. 1, pp. 42–45.

de Groot, R. S. 1983. "Tourism and Conservation in the Galápagos Islands." *Biological Conservation*, vol. 26, pp. 291–300.

Farrell, B. H. 1990. "Sustainable Development: Whatever Happened to Hana?" *Cultural Survival Quarterly*, vol. 14, no. 2, pp. 25–29.

Godfrey, G. 1990. "Tourism Development Should Involve Belizeans at Every Level." *Belize Today*, vol. 4, no. 2, pp. 9–11.

Goering, P. G. 1990. "The Response to Tourism in Ladakh." *Cultural Survival Quarterly*, vol. 14, no. 1, pp. 20–25.

Hartup, B. 1989. "An Alternative Conservation Model for Tropical Areas: The Community Baboon Sanctuary." Master of Science Thesis, University of Wisconsin, Madison.

Horwich, R. H. 1988. "The Community Baboon Sanctuary: An Approach to the Conservation of Private Lands, Belize," in J. Gradwohl and R. Greenberg, eds. *Saving the Tropical Forests*. London: Earthscan Publications, Ltd.

———. 1990. "How to Develop a Community Sanctuary: An Experimental Approach to the Conservation of Private Lands." *Oryx*, vol. 24, pp. 95–102.

Horwich, R. H. and J. Lyon, 1988. "Experimental Technique for the Conservation of Private Lands." *Journal of Medical Primatology*, vol. 17, no. 3, pp. 169–76.

————. 1990. A *Belizean Rain Forest: The Community Baboon Sanctuary*. Gays Mills, Wisc.: Orang-utan Press.

————. 1991. "Proposal For a Multiple Land Use System For The Community Manatee Reserve." Manuscript.

————. In press. "Multi-Level Conservation-Education at the Community Baboon Sanctuary, Belize," in S. K. Jacobson ed. *Wildlife Conservation: International Case Studies of Education and Communication Programs*. New York: Columbia University Press.

Howe, J. 1982. "Kindling Self-Determination Among the Kuna." *Cultural Survival Quarterly*, vol. 6, no. 3, pp. 15–17.

Lippold, L. Personal communication.

Lyon, J. 1986. "Land Use Within the Black Howler Monkey Sanctuary, Belize, Central America: Current and Historical Impacts On Vegetation." Manuscript.

Moll, D. 1986. "The Distribution, Status, and Level of Exploitation of the Freshwater Turtle *Dermatemys Mawei* in Belize, Central America." *Biological Conservation*, vol. 35, pp. 87–96.

Moulin, C. L. 1980. "Plan for Ecological and Cultural Tourism Involving Participation of Local Population and Associations," in D. E. Hawkins, E. L. Shafer and J. M. Rovelstad, eds. *Tourism Planning and Development Issues*. Washington, D.C.: George Washington University.

Passoff, M. 1991. "Ecotourism Re-Examined." *Earth Island Journal*, vol. 6, no. 2, pp. 28–29.

Perez, L. A. 1980. "Tourism Underdevelops Tropical Islands," in I. Vogeler and A. R. de Souza, eds. *Dialectics of Third World Development*. Montclair, N.J.: Allanheld, Osmun and Company.

Peters, J. 1991. "A Participatory Action Research Approach for Ecotourism Development in the Ranomafana National Park, Madagascar," in J. A. Kusler, ed. *Ecotourism and Resource Conservation*, vol. 1. Ecotourism and Resource Conservation Project.

Polit, J. P. 1991. "Ecotourism: Proposals and Reflections for a Community Development and Conservation Project," in J. A. Kusler, ed. *Ecotourism and Resource Conservation*, vol. 1. Ecotourism and Resource Conservation Project.

Puntenney, P. J. 1990. "Defining Solutions: The Annapurna Experience." *Cultural Survival Quarterly*, vol. 14, no. 2, pp. 9–14.

Saglio, C. 1979. "Tourism for Discovery: A Project in Lower Casamance, Senegal," in E. de Kadt, ed. *Tourism: Passport to Development?* Oxford: Oxford University Press.

Tambiah, C. R. 1991. "Integrating Tourists, Local Communities, and Sea Turtles: Facilitating Sustainable Programs," in J. A. Kusler, ed. *Ecotourism and Resource Conservation*, vol. 1. Ecotourism and Resource Conservation Project.

Yamauchi, P. E. 1984. "Guatemalan Tourism and the Efficacy of Wage Employment in Panajachel." *Annals of Tourism Research*, vol. 11, pp. 557–572.

Editors and Contributors

EDITORS

Kreg Lindberg is a research associate for The Ecotourism Society and a graduate research assistant for the Department of Forest Resources at Oregon State University. He has worked for various conservation organizations in the U.S. and abroad. In addition, he has written several papers and reports on ecotourism economics, including *Policies for Maximizing Nature Tourism's Ecological and Economic Benefits*, published by the World Resources Institute. He can be contacted through: The Ecotourism Society, P.O. Box 755, North Bennington, VT 05257, USA; Tel. 802-447-2121; FAX 802-447-2122.

Donald E. Hawkins is Professor of Tourism Studies and Director of The International Institute of Tourism Studies at the George Washington University in Washington, D.C. He recently served as Director of the US-Venezuela Tourism Project and the US-Argentina Tourism Project, both funded by the U.S. Trade and Development Agency. He is the author of more than 100 publications, including *Tourism in Contemporary Society* (Prentice-Hall), General Editor of the Tourism and Commercial Recreation Professional Reference and Textbook Series (Van Nostrand Reinhold), Co-editor and Chief of the *World Travel and Tourism Review* (CAB International) Volume I-III, and the Environmental Classroom (Prentice-Hall). He can be contacted at: The George Washington University, 817 23rd St. N.W., Washington, D.C. 20052; Tel. 202-994-7087; Fax 202-994-1420.

CONTRIBUTORS

David L. Andersen, A.I.A., is the founder of the Andersen Group Architects, Ltd., a Minneapolis-based architectural firm. He has served on the Professional Advisory Board of Iowa State University and is past president of the Minneapolis Chapter of the American Institute of Architects. Mr. Andersen frequently writes and lectures on the subject of ecotourism facility design, and he is a member of The Ecotourism Society. The Andersen Group Architects, Ltd., has become a recognized leader in ecotourism facility design in Central America. The firm is currently involved in the design of ecotourism facilities worldwide. For more information contact: Andersen Group Architects, Ltd., Suite 211, 7601 Wayzata Boulevard, Minneapolis, Minnesota 55426, USA; Tel. 612-593-0950; FAX 612-593-0033.

Sylvie Blangy is an ecotourism consultant and is currently coordinating and editing a special issue of the journal *Espaces* on "Tourism and the Environment in Europe." She is also conducting training programs and feasibility and market studies for the French Departments of Tourism and Environment in French territories such as Guyana, Guadeloupe, Martinique, and the Reunion Islands. She spent two years conducting research on nature tourism codes of ethics, guidelines, and minimum impact policies for the Discovery Tours program of the American Museum of Natural History. Her address is: 123, Rue de la Carrierasse, 34090 Montpellier, France; Tel. and FAX: 67 52 09 94; Email: blangy@frmop22.bitnet.

Elizabeth Boo is the Ecotourism Program Officer for World Wildlife Fund–US, where she has been working since 1986. She has written several reports and papers on ecotourism, including *Ecotourism: The Potentials and Pitfalls*, published by WWF. She holds an M.A. in international affairs from George Washington University, with a concentration in economic development of Latin America. She can be contacted at: World Wildlife Fund, 1250 24th Street NW, Washington, D.C. 20037, USA; Tel. 202-778-9624; FAX 202-293-9211.

Katrina Brandon is a senior fellow at the World Wildlife Fund and a consultant on biodiversity policy, most recently for The Rockefeller Foundation and the Policy and Research Division of the World Bank's Environment Department. Since 1987 Dr. Brandon has worked at the World Wildlife Fund on policies and projects designed to link conservation with development. She coordinated a program in four Latin American countries that promoted sustainable development by incorporating environmental concerns into economic decision making. She is co-author of a World Bank study entitled *People and Parks: Linking Protected Area Management With Local Communities* and co-editor of the April 1992 volume of *World Development* on "Linking Environment and Development." She can be contacted at: World Wildlife Fund, 1250 24th Street, NW, Washington, D.C. 20037, USA, Tel. 202-293-4800, FAX 202-293-9211.

Héctor Ceballos-Lascuráin is the International Union for the Conservation of Nature's (IUCN) Ecotourism Program Coordinator. He was the coordinator of the IVth World Congress on National Parks and Protected Areas attended by more than 1,800 participants from 130 countries in Caracas, Venezuela in 1992. Ceballos-Lascuráin was a consultant to WWF-US on the Latin American Ecotourism Study published in *Ecotourism: The Potentials and Pitfalls* and has lectured on ecotourism at international conferences worldwide. He is a founding partner of ECOTOURS, the first ecotourism tour operation in Mexico. He can be contacted at: The IUCN Ecotourism Program, Camino al Ajusco 551,Tepapan, Xochimilco 16020 México, D.F., México; Tel. 525-676-8734, FAX 525-676-5285.

Megan Epler Wood is the Executive Director of The Ecotourism Society, which she founded in 1990 with the help of advisors from around the world. She holds an M.S. in wildlife biology from Iowa State University and worked for World Wildlife Fund in the 1980s. She received a Fulbright award in 1989 to document wildlife and conservation projects in the rain forests of Colombia. Ms. Epler Wood is a professional documentary filmmaker who has produced films and television programs on environmental subjects for World Wildlife Fund, the National Audubon Society, and National Geographic. Her most recent documentary was a National Audubon Special titled "The Environmental Tourist," broadcast on WTBS and PBS in 1992.

Dolores Godfrey worked from 1990 to 1992 as executive director of the Belize Audubon Society (BAS), Belize City, Belize. The Community Baboon Sanctuary and the Cockscomb Basin Wildlife Sanctuary were under BAS administration. Her work in these areas was both challenging and rewarding. It inspired and sustained her interest in community participation in resource management. Currently she is working on a master's degree in resource conservation at the University of Montana, Missoula, Montana, USA.

Robert H. Horwich received his Ph.D. in 1967 from the University of Maryland and worked in a postdoctoral position in India with the Smithsonian Institution. Based on his research on attachment processes in infant development in birds and mammals, he developed a successful method for reintroducing young cranes into the wild. He has studied primate behavior in India and Central America since 1967 and has worked as an independent researcher and conservationist since 1974. Working with community sanctuaries in Belize and Wisconsin since 1984, he was instrumental in establishing the Community Baboon Sanctuary in Belize. He is currently developing and coordinating the Manatee Community Reserve project in Belize. His address is: Community Conservation Consultants/Howlers Forever, RD 1, Box 96, Gays Mills, Wisconsin 54631, USA.

Richard M. Huber, Jr. works in the environment division of The World Bank Latin America department. Mr. Huber served as a project chief for seven years in Trinidad and Tobago, and Grenada, West Indies for the Organization of American States Department of Regional Development and Environment. He served two years as the director of the Urban Park Rangers in the City of New York Department of Parks and Recreation and served six years in Latin America as a Peace Corps volunteer and consultant. He holds a Master of Forest Science from Yale University.

Jonathan Lyon is currently working on his Ph.D. at Pennsylvania State College, studying the effects of acid rain on U.S. forests. He has researched prairie and wetland restoration in Wisconsin as well as studied tropical rain forest succession following slash-and-burn agriculture at the Community Baboon Sanctuary in Belize. He has been working on community sanctuaries since 1985; his work has provided a basis for the establishment of the Community Baboon Sanctuary and the land management plan for the Manatee Community Reserve.

Dail Murray teaches cultural anthropology and sociology at Viterbo College in Wisconsin and is currently completing a Ph.D. in cultural anthropology from the University of Wisconsin-Madison. She has conducted field research among the Coast Salish Indians and the Old Order Amish communities in the U.S. She helped publicize the Community Baboon Sanctuary during its initial phase.

Ernest Saqui has been the director of the Cockscomb Basin Wildlife Sanctuary in Belize since 1987. He is involved in several community organizations, is the chairman of the Maya Center Village Council, and was instrumental in establishing the women's group in Maya Center. He graduated from the Belize Teachers College.

George N. Wallace is an associate professor at Colorado State University in the Department of Recreation Resources and Landscape Architecture, College of Natural Resources. He teaches courses in wilderness management, wildland ecosystem planning, social science for the natural resource manager, as well as short courses for protected area managers in Latin America. He has worked in Latin America since 1967 and performs research on ecotourism, environmental interpretation, and threats to wildlands. He provides technical assistance to wildland areas in Mexico, Central America, and South America, as well as U.S. public land management agencies. For more information contact: George Wallace, Colorado State University, Forestry Building, Room 238, Fort Collins, CO, 80523, USA.

David Western, The Ecotourism Society's first president, has performed studies on the impacts of wildlife tourism on natural areas for over 15 years. He conducted pioneer research in Kenya's Amboseli National Park, which established the importance of making local people the beneficiaries of wildlife tourism. He has consulted on tourism in natural areas around the world and continues to conduct research and policy analysis in Kenya. He heads the Nairobi office of Wildlife Conservation International, P.O. Box 62844, Nairobi, Kenya; Tel. 221699; FAX 215169.

Country and Site Index

COUNTRIES

SITES